# BASEBALL'S
# GREATEST
# MVPs

The most spectacular and dominant single-season performances in Major League Baseball history.

Baseball Insiders Library®

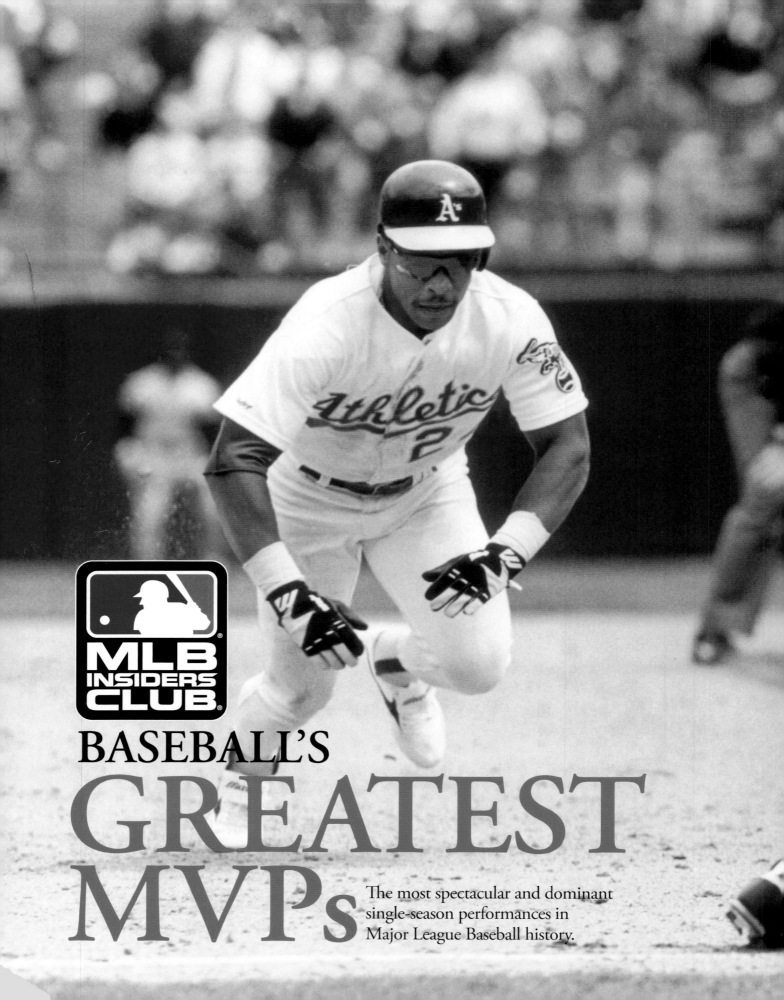

# MLB INSIDERS CLUB

# BASEBALL'S
# GREATEST
# MVPs

The most spectacular and dominant
single-season performances in
Major League Baseball history.

# BASEBALL'S GREATEST MVPs  by Dan Rosen

*The most spectacular and dominant single-season performances in Major League Baseball history.*

Printed in 2013

## About the Author

*Dan Rosen is a freelance writer and editor based in New York. He has worked as a project editor for Major League Baseball Publishing, and is the author of* The Treasures of Major League Baseball, *an officially licensed book cataloging Major League Baseball history and memorabilia.*

## Major League Baseball Properties

**Vice President, Publishing**
Donald S. Hintze

**Editorial Director**
Mike McCormick

**Publications Art Director**
Faith M. Rittenberg

**Senior Production Manager**
Claire Walsh

**Associate Editor**
Jon Schwartz

**Associate Art Director**
Melanie Posner

**Senior Publishing Coordinator**
Anamika Chakrabarty

**Project Assistant Editors**
Chris Greenberg, Jodie Jordan

**Editorial Intern**
Karl de Vries

## Major League Baseball Photos

**Director**
Rich Pilling

**Photo Editor**
Paul Cunningham

## MLB Insiders Club

**Creative Director**
Tom Carpenter

**Managing Editor**
Jen Weaverling

**Prepress**
Wendy Holdman
Gina Germ

MLB Insiders Club
12301 Whitewater Drive
Minnetonka, MN 55343

# TABLE OF CONTENTS

BASEBALL'S BEST HAVE A CERTAIN SWAGGER ABOUT them when the going is good. For a pitcher, it's a faith in one's stuff. It's the "Here's my best pitch, hit it if you can" bravado that leaves opposing lineups buckling at the plate. For a batter, it's the slow-motion groove, when even a triple-digit heater seems like it's sitting up on a tee, ready to meet the fat part of the bat.

In 1999, Chipper Jones experienced that groove for the Atlanta Braves. For a week in mid-April, the third baseman hit five homers and recorded 13 RBI to go along with a .423 average. "If they miss their spot," Jones said of opposing pitchers during such a hot streak, "you're gonna make 'em pay for it."

Fans eat up that type of run, reveling in its perfection. For Joe DiMaggio's 56 in 1941 or Sandy Koufax's perfect nine in 1965, they sat glued to their radios. "No one who was around here in 1967 will ever forget," wrote *The Boston Globe* of left fielder Carl Yastrzemski's magical campaign in Beantown.

Players rarely ride such a wave for an entire season, though. "The Zone," as it's so frequently referred to, can be short-lived. Pitches that looked like beach balls from the batter's box one day can shrink to golf ball size the next. And curveballs that seemed to snap into the dirt suddenly hang over the plate for anyone to drive.

The Most Valuable Players handle highs and lows better than the rest. Of course, they experience the hot streaks, some of historic proportions. But they also weather the down times, making adjustments before a full-blown slump overtakes them.

In July 1965, after a torrid first few months, Willie Mays collected just 18 hits and two home runs in 78 at-bats (for a .231 mark). But as the calendar flipped, he came back around to his otherworldly self. In August, he would hit .363 with an amazing 17 longballs, helping the San Francisco Giants move from third to second place in the National League. Come season's end, Mays was honored with his second NL MVP Award.

But a hot week, a hot month or even a hot half-season does not make an MVP campaign. It's helping your ballclub, adjustments and all, over the course of a grueling 162 games. Such MVP efforts come in all shapes and sizes, from giant sluggers to contact hitters and sleek speedsters, from overpowering relievers to crafty starters, nimble defensemen and everything in between. There are stories from more than 100 MVP seasons in the pages that follow, because there's no set mold for such a year, no statistical benchmark. All it takes is a whole lot of good days, playing one's own particular style at its very best and the inner strength to minimize the bad bits that come up along the way — longevity worth remembering.

Cobb (sliding)

# chapter 1
# THE ORIGINALS

*Today's Most Valuable Player Award, voted on by the Baseball Writers' Association of America, was born in 1931. But it wasn't the first of its kind. The Chalmers Motor Company of Detroit introduced the Chalmers Award in 1911, and presented each league's best with an automobile — the Tigers' Ty Cobb and the Cubs' Frank Schulte were the first winners. There would be just six more recipients, as the prize folded after 1914, to be followed by the also short-lived League Awards. Although the exact hardware given to the game's best may have been inconsistent, on-field performances were anything but.*

## TY COBB 1911 (AL)

ENTERING SEPTEMBER 1911, TY COBB WAS in a tight race with Joe Jackson for the AL batting crown. When Cobb's Tigers arrived in Cleveland for a late-season series with Jackson's Naps, Cobb showed his legendary competitive fire and approached Jackson during batting practice.

"Kid, it's too bad you didn't come up in the other league," witnesses recalled Cobb saying.

"Why?" Jackson asked. "I'm doin' all right in this one, ain't I?"

"Yeah," quipped Cobb, "but if you'd come up in the National League, you could have led the league in hitting."

Good to his brash word, Cobb finished 12 points ahead of Jackson in arguably the finest year of his Hall of Fame career. That winter Cobb was given a Chalmers Award as the AL MVP. Popular opinion maintained that the Award was created by the Detroit company simply to honor Cobb, the local hero.

Having led the league in almost every statistic but friends, Cobb was a deserving recipient. He finished the campaign with a stunning .420 average (to Jackson's .408), 248 hits and 127 RBI. At one point, Cobb compiled a then-AL-record 40-game hit streak.

The left-handed Cobb was known to choke up on the bat and part his hands for control. It seemed as if he could put the ball anywhere he wanted — most often, where fielders weren't standing. In fact, he was so comfortable at the plate that he struck out swinging just twice the whole summer of 1911.

Cobb was also a terror on the basepaths, taking bases by force if necessary. He stole a Big-League-record 83 bags in 1911. No one, it seemed, could stand in Cobb's way.

| HR | RBI | AVG | HITS |
|----|-----|------|------|
| 8 | 127 | .420 | 248 |

| HR | RBI | AVG | G |
|----|-----|-----|-----|
| 47 | 175 | .373 | 155 |

## LOU GEHRIG 1927 (AL)

FEW SQUADS IN BASEBALL HISTORY enjoyed fireworks from their lineup quite like the 1927 Yankees — considered by many to be the greatest team ever. The club's stars were outfielder Babe Ruth, who hit a single-season-record-setting 60 home runs that year, and first baseman Lou Gehrig.

Ruth and Gehrig were described as night and day. "Whereas the Babe would arrive at Yankee Stadium on game day by bringing his convertible to a screeching stop at the main gate," Shirley Povich later wrote in *The Washington Post*, "the shy Gehrig parked his own car three blocks from the park and found his way into the stadium through a side gate."

In the batter's box, though, the two found common ground. For much of 1927, Gehrig hung with Ruth on the power chart. After knocking two homers in early August, the New York native led the pair, 38 to 35. Although Ruth would surpass his total of 47, Gehrig finished ahead of Ruth in virtually ever other category. He hit .373 to the Babe's .356 and drove in a then-record 175 runs to Ruth's 164.

But Gehrig's clear superiority was not necessary. Ruth was ineligible to win the League Award. By rule, no one could get it twice, and the Babe captured the honor in 1923. That made Gehrig, who often was forced to fade into Ruth's shadow, the runaway winner.

GEHRIG'S GLOVE

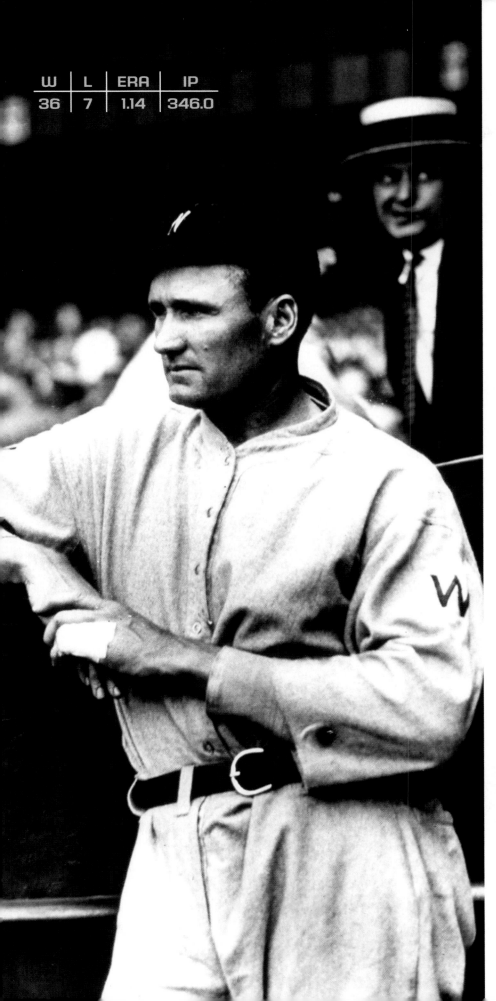

| W | L | ERA | IP |
|---|---|-----|-----|
| 36 | 7 | 1.14 | 346.0 |

## WALTER JOHNSON
### 1913 (AL)

FOR ONCE, WALTER JOHNSON had some help. During the pitcher's first five years in the Majors (from 1907–11), the Washington Senators didn't sniff the .500 mark, twice dropping 100 games in a campaign. That changed in 1912, with the arrival of Manager Clark Griffith. For a few years the Senators were contenders. Finally, surrounded by help, Johnson, a future Hall of Famer, took full advantage. In 1913 he won a career-high 36 games (40 percent of the team's 90 wins) and the AL Chalmers Award.

There was no secret to his success. Johnson was nearly unbeatable because he hurled, with notable ease, one of the game's all-time greatest fastballs. "You hardly saw the ball at all," Tigers Hall of Famer Sam Crawford once said. "But you heard it. Swoosh, and it would smack into the catcher's mitt."

It was his only pitch, but that didn't seem to matter — he rode it to stardom. During his first decade in the Big Leagues, his ERA rarely climbed above 2.00.

In 1913 it was 1.14, helped by a 56-inning scoreless streak. Washington won five 1-0 decisions with Johnson on the hill that season and finished in second place.

"In his best years," statistician Bill James once wrote of Johnson, "he had records that were as good as anybody for teams that weren't as good as anybody's." True in most seasons, it was not the case in 1913 when, thanks largely to Johnson's fastball, the Senators finally found a way to compete.

## BABE RUTH 1923 (AL)

| HR | RBI | AVG | SLG |
|----|-----|------|------|
| 41 | 131 | .393 | .764 |

THE 1922 SEASON WAS A DISAPPOINTING ONE BY BABE Ruth's lofty standards. His numbers dipped significantly. He fought with umpires and fans, and earned multiple suspensions. He indulged in the excess of Gotham's nightlife. At a ritzy banquet before the 1923 campaign got under way, New York Assemblyman (and future Mayor) Jimmy Walker pleaded with the great Yankees slugger to curb his detrimental off-the-field activities and take care of his body. "So help me Jim, I will," a sobbing Sultan of Swat responded.

Ruth was no stranger to adversity. As a kid in Baltimore, he lost his mother, and after making his share of adolescent trouble, was sent to a reform school to right himself.

Accustomed to overcoming challenges, Ruth began the 1923 season looking like a man on a mission. He was leaner, and he set about answering the Assemblyman's bell.

The stage for his return to dominance couldn't have been set more perfectly than it was on April 18 when the Bronx Bombers opened the doors to their new park, Yankee Stadium. The Boston Red Sox, Ruth's old team, were the visitors. Ruth said according to the *Daily News* that he would "give a year of my life if I can hit a home run in the first game in this new park."

In the third inning, his prayers were answered. Ruth came to bat with two men on and walloped one low and hard over the right-field screen. It was an emphatic start to Ruth's statement season. He went on to hit .393, driving in 131 runs and walking an eye-popping 170 times. Most would surely consider his mission accomplished.

According to *The Daily News*, the 36-inch bat Ruth used to hit his famous homer at Yankee Stadium's Grand Opening was sold for a record $1.265 million in 2004.

| HR | RBI | AVG | SLG |
|---|---|---|---|
| 39 | 143 | .403 | .756 |

## ROGERS HORNSBY 1925 (NL)

A RIVAL TO TY COBB IN BOTH HITTING PROWESS and ornery behavior, Rogers Hornsby won the Triple Crown in 1925. With time running out on the season, though, it looked like he might fall short of the .400 mark (a milestone he reached in two of the previous three seasons). Standing at .389 on Sept. 15, the St. Louis star went 18 for 29 to finish the campaign at .403.

As fine a batter as ever laced up spikes, Hornsby was serious about his work. He avoided the movies and reading during the season for fear those leisure activities would affect his batting eye. He didn't drink, smoke or dance either. And by 1925, Hornsby was the second-highest paid ballplayer, behind only Babe Ruth.

Unlike Ruth, he earned his salary with more than his bat. On Memorial Day, with the Cardinals 11 games below .500, Team President Sam Breadon dismissed Branch Rickey in between games of a double header, and installed Hornsby as player-manager. St. Louis finished 77-76. The next year, with Hornsby at the helm and at the plate, they won the World Series.

But his prickly personality undoubtedly made him tough to play for. Hornsby was incredibly blunt in his evaluations of players. Shortstop Travis Jackson, who played for Hornsby as a Giant, told *Sports Illustrated*, "He had a good way of making everybody irritated."

| HR | RBI | AVG | HITS |
|---|---|---|---|
| 8 | 105 | .420 | 246 |

## GEORGE SISLER
### 1922 (AL)

YEARS BEFORE JOE DiMAGGIO HIT in 56 straight games for the Yankees, there was George Sisler, whose hit-streak heroics often go unmentioned. In 1922, Sisler hit in a then-record 41 straight during his MVP year with the St. Louis Browns.

Far from a fluke, his record-breaking parade came at the conclusion of a .420 season (a few seasons after notching 257 hits in 1920, a record until 2004). He often extended his streak with multi-hit games.

A serious arm injury in mid-September likely derailed the streak, but little could take away from his overall season. In addition to his characteristically stellar play at first base, Sisler led the league in batting average (.420), hits (246), runs (134), triples (18) and stolen bases (51). And he carried the Browns, so often an afterthought in the AL and even in their own city (where they played second fiddle to the Cardinals), to a second-place finish.

"He was a professional with the bat in his hands," said Branch Rickey, Sisler's coach at the University of Michigan who brought him to the Majors as a pitcher after graduation in 1915. "He never stopped thinking. He was a menace every time he stepped to the plate."

Today, "Gorgeous George," a 1939 Hall of Fame inductee, gets lost in most discussions of the all-time greatest players. "Sisler was a great hitter and first baseman," said fellow Cooperstown honoree Eddie Collins, "but he was too quiet and clean-living to win headlines."

15

| HR | RBI | AVG | HITS |
|----|-----|------|------|
| 10 | 90  | .383 | 222  |

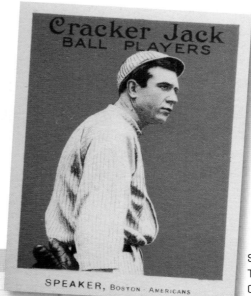

SPEAKER
TRADING
CARD

| CHALMERS AWARD WINNERS (1911–1914) | | | |
|---|---|---|---|
| YEAR | LEAGUE | WINNER | TEAM |
| 1911 | NL | Frank Schulte, OF | Chicago Cubs |
| | AL | Ty Cobb, OF | Detroit Tigers |
| 1912 | NL | Larry Doyle, 2B | New York Giants |
| | AL | Tris Speaker, OF | Boston Red Sox |
| 1913 | NL | Jake Daubert, 1B | Brooklyn Dodgers |
| | AL | Walter Johnson, P | Washington Senators |
| 1914 | NL | Johnny Evers, 2B | Boston Braves |
| | AL | Eddie Collins, 2B | Philadelphia Athletics |

## TRIS SPEAKER 1912 (AL)

THE GREAT TRIS SPEAKER LAUNCHED HIS MVP campaign with a heroic performance on April 20, 1912, following two days of rainouts, at the regular-season debut of Fenway Park. Against the rival High-landers (soon the Yankees) and to the delight of 27,000 fans, Speaker drove home the winning run in the 11th, as his Sox won, 7-6. He finished with 90 RBI on the year, a .383 average and a league-best in doubles (53) and homers (10, to tie Frank Baker).

Although he made plenty of noise with his terrific bat, Speaker was better known for his defense — as a center fielder he had few rivals. Playing 30 to 40 feet behind second base, he used tremendous speed to track down deep balls. But the shallow positioning also allowed forays to the infield, where Speaker could turn unassisted double plays and sneak behind base runners on pickoff plays. With a rocket arm, he tied for the league high for an outfielder with 35 assists in 1912.

Before he learned to corral wayward runners, the Hubbard, Texas, native roped calves, according to the *Houston Chronicle*. As a kid, Speaker was a true cowboy.

Regardless, the 1912 season ended much as it had begun — with late-inning heroics at the plate. In the 10th frame of the eighth and deciding game of the World Series, with his Sox down, 2-1, Speaker fouled a ball toward first. It dropped harmlessly among a swarm of New York Giants. Later in that at-bat, Speaker rapped the game-tying hit and Boston went on to win, 3-2.

AVERAGE TOTALS FOR MVP SEASONS

| HR | RBI | AVG | SLG |
|----|-----|-----|-----|
| 50 | 135 | .311 | .606 |

## chapter 2

# EXTENDED
# DOMINANCE

*The list of baseball's Most Valuable Players is filled with some impressive names. The list of honorees to win multiple awards is even more eye-popping. It takes a truly special talent to follow up one great campaign with another (and in some cases, another and another). These days, the names are mythic. Hall of Famer Jimmie Foxx won three MVPs in the 1930s. St. Louis great Stan Musial won three in the '40s. Joe DiMaggio, Mickey Mantle, Hank Greenberg and Frank Robinson are also members of one of baseball's most elite clubs: the multiple MVP Award winners.*

## ALEX RODRIGUEZ  2003, 2005, 2007 (AL)

SHOULD ONE HAVE TO PLAY ON A WINNING TEAM TO BE CONSIDERED the league's most valuable player? The case of Alex Rodriguez, star of the last-place Texas Rangers, roused this debate in 2003. A cellar dweller had garnered the MVP hardware just once: Andre Dawson of the downtrodden Cubs took home the prize in 1987.

For years, Rodriguez had been putting his once-in-a-generation talent on display, only to be overlooked come award season. While injuries kept 2003 from being his finest campaign, it was still off-the-charts. In August he launched 15 home runs (setting a single-month record for a shortstop), hit .340 and knocked in 31 runs. That the Rangers were 20 games out of first place when the month began was hardly his fault. "He makes the people better around him," his then-hitting-coach Rudy Jaramillo told the *Fort Worth Star-Telegram.*

The following season, Rodriguez moved to New York (and to third base). With A-Rod, the Yankees won division titles in three of his first four years in pinstripes. Unburdened by the reluctance to pick a winner from a loser, voters gave Rodriguez MVP honors in 2005 and '07. The latter may have been his best season. He hit six homers in the first seven games and finished with a Major League-best 54. He added career highs in runs (143) and RBI (156). The Yankees also reached the playoffs as the AL Wild Card and Rodriguez garnered 26 out of 28 first-place MVP votes.

RODRIGUEZ'S HELMET

| AVERAGE TOTALS FOR MVP SEASONS | | | |
|---|---|---|---|
| HR | RBI | AVG | SLG |
| 46 | 136 | .308 | .605 |

## ERNIE BANKS 1958, 1959 (NL)

FOR TWO YEARS, MR. CUB WAS ALSO MR. MVP. HALL of Famer Ernie Banks' stunning talent and sunny disposition made him a Wrigley Field favorite during his 19 seasons in the Windy City. Banks won the award in back-to-back years in the late 1950s. Fittingly, his success during those seasons was due in large part to his comfort playing in the "Friendly Confines" on the north side of Chicago. Banks hit .331 at home in 1958 and '59, belting 54 homers over the famous ivy-covered walls.

A Dallas native, Banks became the first African-American to play for the Cubs. When he stepped out of the dugout prior to his first game in 1953, he was greeted by Jackie Robinson, in town with the visiting Dodgers. "Congratulations," Robinson beamed. "I'm glad to have you here. It's terrific."

Cubs fans immediately fell in love with Banks', "Let's play two!" attitude. "To play ball so well, he had to have been a fierce competitor driven by an inner intensity," wrote *The Chicago Sun-Times*, "but what he revealed to the fans — and it never felt anything but genuine — was a sunny kindness."

Although Chicago finished in fifth place in both of Banks' MVP campaigns, few could doubt the shortstop's value. Quipped Jimmie Dykes, the former-player-turned-manager: "Without him, the Cubs would finish in Albuquerque."

## FRANK THOMAS
## 1993, 1994 (AL)

ALTHOUGH IT TOOK A FEW YEARS, the South Side eventually got a chance to cheer for a dominant MVP of its own. Frank Thomas arrived in Chicago late in the 1990 season after being called up from the Double-A Birmingham Barons. He was a massive 22-year-old slugger with plate discipline beyond his years. Thomas walked more than 100 times in each of his first eight full Big League seasons. He took 112 free passes in 1993, the first of his two MVP campaigns.

When a pitcher was brave enough — or foolish enough — to throw a ball anywhere near the strike zone, Thomas teed off. His 41 home runs in 1993 pushed the White Sox to the top of the AL West. He hit 38 dingers in 113 games in 1994, a season shortened by a players strike.

But it was his patience in those MVP campaigns that continually impressed teammates and coaches. "We got a game the other day," then-Chicago-hitting coach Walter Hriniak said in May of the 1994 season, "and the count's 2 and 0, there's nobody on, and we've got a left-handed pitcher that isn't going to give in to Frank. Most guys who hit a lot of home runs would try to pull the next pitch out of the ballpark. But Frank knew the guy wasn't going to give him that type of pitch, that he was going to give him this type of pitch — a fastball moving away. Frank shot a single to right field." Thomas would hit an impressive .353 that season, taking the American League's top individual honor for a second straight year.

## TED WILLIAMS  1946, 1949 (AL)

HAVING MISSED THREE SEASONS TO SERVE IN THE armed forces, Boston's Ted Williams began the 1946 season like he was making up for lost time. He belted a mammoth home run on Opening Day at Washington's Griffith Stadium and didn't look back, running away with his first MVP Award.

Williams even dominated the All-Star Game that season, which was played at Fenway Park, going 4 for 4 at the plate, with two home runs. One longball came against Pirates right-hander Rip Sewell, who challenged the Splendid Splinter with his famous "eephus" pitch (essentially an exaggerated lob). "It was a good one, dropping right down the chute for a strike," Sewell would tell *The Boston Globe* years later. "He took a couple of steps on it — which was the right way to attack that pitch, incidentally — and he hit it right out of there. And I mean he hit it."

After watching Williams rack up eight RBI in the first game of a July double-header against the Cleveland Indians, player-manager Lou Boudreau shifted his infielders and two of his outfielders to the right side of the diamond. Sure enough, Williams' sharp grounder in the third inning of Game 2 turned into an easy out. But Williams got the last laugh, clinching the

**AVERAGE TOTALS FOR MVP SEASONS**

| HR | RBI | AVG | SLG |
| --- | --- | --- | --- |
| 41 | 141 | .343 | .658 |

pennant with an inside-the-park home run on Sept. 13. It was an opposite-field shot, and it caught the Indians' shifted defense completely out of position.

Williams was MVP again in 1949, when he reached career highs in home runs (43) and RBI (159). During one stretch, Williams reached base in 84 straight games.

AVERAGE TOTALS FOR MVP SEASONS

| HR | RBI | AVG | SLG |
|----|-----|-----|-----|
| 39 | 110 | .295 | .600 |

## MIKE SCHMIDT  1980, 1981, 1986 (NL)

MIKE SCHMIDT FINALLY SEEMED AT EASE. IT WAS 1982, the third baseman's 10th season with the Philadelphia Phillies, and the weight of expectations appeared lifted from his shoulders. "The level I play the game at now is one that not many players have played it at," Schmidt admitted at Spring Training.

Few could argue. His first seven seasons had been well above average, but he had elevated his game to another stratosphere by

1982, having won back-to-back MVP Awards in 1980 and '81 (and a World Series ring in '80). Schmidt led the league in OPS and RBI in both seasons, which went along with Gold Glove defense.

"Mike was the best player in the league three or four days a week when I got there," said ex-teammate Pete Rose, who arrived in Philadelphia in 1979. "By the time I left, he had learned to be the best seven days a week."

## HAL NEWHOUSER  1944, 1945 (AL)

HAL NEWHOUSER DID NOT SERVE IN THE ARMED forces during World War II. He volunteered but was deferred because of a heart condition. For years people condescendingly called him a "wartime player" since his two MVP Awards with the Tigers came in 1944 and 1945, when many of the game's greats were overseas and out of action.

But no one could contest that he was dominant during the war years, going 54-18 for Detroit. On the final day of the regular season in 1945, with the Tigers in need of a victory to reach the World Series, Newhouser came in as a reliever. He scratched his way out of a bases-loaded jam, and Detroit rallied to reach the Fall Classic. In the Series, he won Games 5 and 7 (the latter a 10-strikeout, complete game) to give the Tigers the title.

### AVERAGE TOTALS FOR MVP SEASONS

| W | L | ERA | IP |
|---|---|-----|-----|
| 27 | 9 | 2.01 | 313 |

A lefty throwing high heat, he attracted the Tigers' attention when he was growing up in Detroit. "He became a beautiful pitcher," said Ted Williams, a member of the Veterans Committee that elected Newhouser to the Hall of Fame decades after his retirement. According to Williams, "Newhouser had everything. Joe Cronin always said he would have won in any era."

Schmidt added a third MVP Award in 1986. Three years later, he wrapped up arguably the greatest career ever by a third baseman. That his home fans had occasionally (and infamously) booed him was no black mark on his record. After all, this was the town that once booed Santa Claus. "The man's only crime," wrote Dave Kindred, after Schmidt retired, "was to come to the ballpark with a gift so large he made hard things look easy."

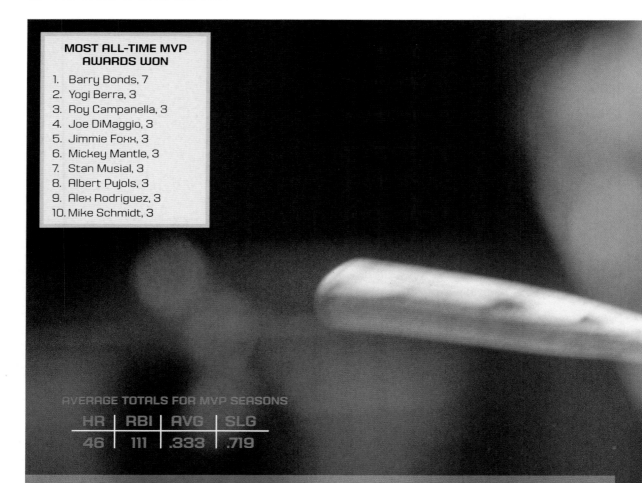

**MOST ALL-TIME MVP AWARDS WON**

1. Barry Bonds, 7
2. Yogi Berra, 3
3. Roy Campanella, 3
4. Joe DiMaggio, 3
5. Jimmie Foxx, 3
6. Mickey Mantle, 3
7. Stan Musial, 3
8. Albert Pujols, 3
9. Alex Rodriguez, 3
10. Mike Schmidt, 3

AVERAGE TOTALS FOR MVP SEASONS

| HR | RBI | AVG | SLG |
|---|---|---|---|
| 46 | 111 | .333 | .719 |

## BARRY BONDS 1990, 1992, 1993, 2001, 2002, 2003, 2004 (NL)

WHEN IT COMES TO THE MVP AWARD, there's dominance and then there's Barry Bonds, who has won so many awards that he seems worthy of his own category all together.

Bonds began collecting accolades in 1990 as a member of the Pittsburgh Pirates. The formula seemed simple enough: Gold Glove defense in left field, plus more than 40 steals, plus a .300 average, plus 30-something home runs, equals trophy. But soon the league tried to change that equation.

By 1993, Bonds' first season with the San Francisco Giants, his opponents (including even the NL's worst team) were wary of letting the game's best beat them. In one three-game series in July, the lowly Mets walked Bonds in each of the games, twice intentionally. And although San Francisco took two of the contests, some in the local media awarded the Mets something of a moral victory for their containment

of the perennial MVP. "You try to think of him as just one batter, but he is so dangerous," New York's rookie starter Dave Telgheder told *Newsday*. "He can hit the ball out of the yard, or he can get on and steal second and third." Because of the many ways he could beat a pitcher, Bonds was intentionally walked 43 times in 1993, en route to his third MVP honor.

Over the years the idea of pitching to the lefty slugger got even scarier. By the early 2000s, it seemed impossible to slip a strike past his quick, powerful stroke. The MVP Awards kept coming — he won in 2001, 2002, 2003 and 2004. In 2001, he set a single-season record with 73 home runs. In 2004, he was intentionally walked 120 times, but still managed to lead the league in slugging and knock in 101 runs, taking his fourth consecutive trophy. ESPN's Jayson Stark summed it up that fall, saying, "The league Barry Bonds plays in is a league all his own."

Berra (right)

| AVERAGE TOTALS FOR MVP SEASONS | | | |
|---|---|---|---|
| HR | RBI | AVG | SLG |
| 25 | 107 | .291 | .483 |

## YOGI BERRA  1951, 1954, 1955 (AL)

THE 1950s WERE AN EXCITING TIME FOR BASEBALL in the Big Apple, particularly behind the plate, where two Hall of Fame backstops were enjoying their prime years. In Brooklyn, Roy Campanella won three National League MVP Awards for the Dodgers, while further north in the Bronx, fan-favorite Yogi Berra kept taking home the hardware.

Years later, when discussing the 1954 Indians (a team that won 111 games), Berra praised second baseman Bobby Avila. "He got the MVP that year, I think," he recalled. "1954? I'm pretty sure. Didn't he?" Actually it was Berra that won the Award in 1954, an honor he earned with a .307 average and 125 RBI. With his

quick bat, Berra could put nearly any pitch in play, striking out just 29 times that season. He was fanned just 20 times the next year with 27 longballs, gathering numbers deemed worthy of his second consecutive MVP nod (and third overall).

Perhaps best known as a source of great quotes (hence the title of one of his books, *I Really Didn't Say Everything I Said*), Berra was a beloved figure in baseball. Historian Bill James laments that Berra's image "as a kind of short, knobby comic-book reader grew larger and larger, and the memory of Yogi Berra as one hell of a catcher kind of drooped into the background." In the mid-1950s, however, MVP voters recognized him as just that.

| AVERAGE TOTALS FOR MVP SEASONS | | | |
|---|---|---|---|
| HR | RBI | AVG | SLG |
| 42 | 123 | .338 | .640 |

## ALBERT PUJOLS  2005, 2008, 2009 (NL)

SINCE PROFESSIONAL BASEBALL TURNED THE calendar to the 21st century, no hitter has dominated the game as emphatically as Albert Pujols. The Cardinals' slugging first baseman spent the first 11 years of his career in the National League, a period that began with Rookie of the Year honors in 2001, ended with his second World Series ring in 2011, and included three NL MVP Awards, nine All-Star Game selections, six Silver Sluggers and two Gold Gloves in between.

The numbers from the first decade of his career are otherworldly. With St. Louis, Pujols posted a season average of 40 homers, 121 RBI, 117 runs, 188 hits and a slash line of .328/.420/.617. His stats only saw a minimal spike in his three MVP years — .338, 42

home runs, 123 RBI, 118 runs, 189 hits — which indicates just how dominant he was, regardless of the accolades he may or may not have received in any given season. Pujols could perform in the clutch, too, leading the Cardinals to World Series titles in 2006 and '11, with a three–home run game in the latter Series.

Pujols' production was as steady as it was powerful. In the eight years with the Cardinals in which he did not win MVP, he never finished outside the top 10 in voting, only once finished outside the top five and was runner-up four times. "You're talking about a guy that year in, year out is head and shoulders above even the elite players," said Mets third baseman David Wright. "It's almost like the bigger the situation, the better he is."

## chapter 3
# LEATHER MEN

*They're not always the most obvious choice for the league's top honor, for their skills have always been hard to quantify with numbers. But baseball's finest defenders save their teams countless runs. In 1959, AL MVP Nellie Fox was a fine offensive player. He hit .306, led the league with 149 singles and drove in 70 runs. Although there were better hitters that year (Detroit's Harvey Kuenn for example), Fox's defense set him above. He was a Gold Glover at second and voters recognized that the pennant-winning White Sox wouldn't have been the same without him. Just one of the game's many defensive-driven MVPs.*

## WILLIE MAYS  1954 (NL)

"THE CATCH" — WILLIE MAYS' BREATH-taking over-the-shoulder grab and throw in Game 1 of the 1954 World Series — is widely considered one of the best defensive plays of all time.

But Mays wasn't sure it was even the best play of his career. For starters, there was a catch against the Dodgers in 1954 (Mays' first MVP campaign), when a sliding snag on the warning track knocked him out. "When I came to, there were two guys there — Jackie Robinson and [Manager] Leo [Durocher]," recalled Mays. "I said I know why Leo is out here. He wants to see if I'm okay. Jackie said, 'I'm out here to see if you caught the ball.' I can't tell you what I told him ... all kinds of names."

A highlight reel in center field, Mays prided himself on being an all-around player. The Hall of Famer combined legendary plate skills with a strong arm and wide range ("He covers center like he had jet shoes," sang The Treniers in "Say Hey" — their ode to Mays). He won 12 Gold Gloves Awards, which ties him with Roberto Clemente for most by an outfielder. In 1954, he had a career-high 448 putouts and cut down 13 base runners.

He also hit .345 — tops in the Majors — raked 41 homers and drove in 110 runs for the Giants (who thanks in part to Mays' Game 1 catch, swept the Indians in the World Series).

| HR | RBI | AVG | FP |
|----|-----|-----|-----|
| 41 | 110 | .345 | .985 |

Mays won his second MVP Award in 1965 when he belted a career-high 52 home runs. The highlight of that season came on Sept. 13 in Houston when Mays hit home run No. 47 on the year and 500 for his career (he would finish with 660). Said former Manager Alvin Dark, "Willie is the best player I ever laid eyes on."

# IVAN RODRIGUEZ 1999 (AL)

| HR | RBI | AVG | FP |
|----|-----|-----|-----|
| 35 | 113 | .332 | .993 |

"IT'S THE BEST SEASON I'VE SEEN, ALL AROUND, BY A CATCHER," ALL-Star backstop Sandy Alomar said of Ivan Rodriguez's 1999 MVP campaign. It was "all around" great because, in addition to his prowess at the plate, Rodriguez played superb defense behind it.

The anchor of the first-place Texas Rangers that year, "Pudge" caught 141 games, striking fear in opposing base runners with his lethal throwing arm. Those speedsters willing to challenge Rodriguez were thrown out more than 50 percent of the time. Not that staying at first was much safer that season — Rodriguez also picked off 10 runners who strayed too far from the bag.

Opposing catchers had a harder time keeping Rodriguez in check; he stole a career-high 25 bases in 1999 and put up personal bests in hits (199), homers (35) — a new record by an AL catcher — and RBI (113) to go with his stellar average (.332). Rodriguez especially dominated in July, August and September when he batted .350 with 22 dingers. On Aug. 15 and 16, he had back-to-back two-homer games, going 7 for 12.

Texas's loss to the Yankees in the Division Series did little to dim the shine of Rodriguez's season. In addition to MVP hardware, Pudge was awarded his eighth Gold Glove. "I've stayed away from saying he's the best catcher ever to play the game," Rangers Manager Johnny Oates said. "I think it's impossible to compare players from different eras because it's different teams, different ballparks. But of the catchers I have seen, there is nobody who throws with him. Nobody."

## GOLD GLOVE RECORDS BY POSITION

| POSITION | PLAYER | AWARDS |
|----------|--------|--------|
| Pitcher | Greg Maddux | 18 |
| Catcher | Ivan Rodriguez* | 13 |
| First Base | Keith Hernandez* | 11 |
| Second Base | Roberto Alomar | 10 |
| Third Base | Brooks Robinson* | 16 |
| Shortstop | Ozzie Smith | 13 |
| Outfield | Roberto Clemente*/ Willie Mays* | 12 |
| | Al Kaline/Andruw Jones/ Ken Griffey Jr.* | 10 |

* denotes MVP winners

| HR | RBI | AVG | FP |
|---|---|---|---|
| 11 | 105 | .344 | .995 |

## KEITH HERNANDEZ
## 1979 (NL)

PETE ROSE APPROACHED KEITH Hernandez during the 1979 season and offered him his unofficial vote for MVP. Willie Stargell did, too. Still, the Cardinals first baseman said in September that he'd be "pleasantly surprised if I get it."

By the end of that month Hernandez had the credentials to go along with the support of his peers. One of the finest fielding first basemen in history, he led the league in putouts at first base, assists, double plays and chances per game that season. Hernandez played far off the bag, and he was aggressive in fielding bunts and charging across the diamond to spoil sacrifices with throws to second or third.

Hernandez also won the batting title in 1979 (with a .344 average), surpassing Rose in a tight race. Extremely proud of this accomplishment, he said that he'd one day tell his grandkids about going toe-to-toe with the legendary Charlie Hustle. By topping Rose, Hernandez became the first infielder to win the batting title and a Gold Glove Award in the same year.

Although Hernandez was never a longball hitter — he cleared the fences just 11 times in 1979 and never hit more then 18 home runs in a single season — he collected 105 RBI and led the Majors with 48 doubles.

In the end, it added up to a "pleasant surprise" for Hernandez, who tied Stargell in the MVP vote and thus shared the honor. In his career, he would win 11 Gold Gloves, the most ever by a first baseman.

| HR | RBI | AVG | SLG |
|----|-----|-----|-----|
| 19 | 84  | .314 | .993 |

SANDBERG'S CAP

## RYNE SANDBERG
## 1984 (NL)

PRIOR TO THE 1983 SEASON, THE Chicago Cubs traded two Minor Leaguers to the Dodgers for third baseman Ron Cey. To make room, the Cubs moved a quiet and talented youngster, Ryne Sandberg — who had played 133 games at the hot corner in 1982 — to second base.

It turned out that Sandberg was a natural right-sider, becoming the first player ever to win a Gold Glove in his first season at a new position. And the next year, Sandberg was better. He had just six errors, including a stretch of 62 games with none. "He would be a Gold Glover at any position he played," his former Manager Jim Frey said. "Give him two weeks anywhere on the field, and you will have one of the best players at that position in the Majors."

He was gifted at the plate, too. On June 23, 1984, with the rival Cardinals at Wrigley, Sandberg went 5 for 6 with two homers and seven RBI. "You could not throw the ball by him inside," said former pitcher and Cubs broadcaster Steve Stone.

He hit .314 with 19 home runs in '84, passing the 15 total from his first *two* years in the Bigs. "What I told him was that on certain pitches I knew he could handle," Frey said, "he should be looking to drive the ball for extra bases, instead of settling for singles." Sandberg finished third in the league in slugging and first in MVP voting.

Robinson got 18 of 20 first-place votes in 1964, finishing comfortably ahead of a pair of Yankees — Mickey Mantle and Elston Howard.

## BROOKS ROBINSON  1964 (AL)

| HR | RBI | AVG | FP |
|----|-----|-----|------|
| 28 | 118 | .317 | .972 |

THEY CALLED BROOKS ROBINSON "THE Human Vacuum Cleaner" for good reason. In 1964, as he did throughout his 23-year career, the Orioles' third baseman played Hoover on the infield dirt, swallowing up groundballs in even the most hard-to-reach places.

"Whenever a new guy would join the bullpen," former Orioles reliever Dick Hall told *The Baltimore Sun*, "he'd watch Brooks for a game or two and say, 'Holy cow, he's as good as they say.'"

"It takes a lot of hard work to be that good," Hall explained. "And no one worked harder than Brooks." Some of it was effort. Some of it was natural ability. Robinson had fast hands and tremendous hand-eye coordination. On the basketball court he was a prodigious rebounder, with a knack for anticipating where the ball would bounce.

He won 16 Gold Gloves including one in '64 when he made just 14 errors. His Gold Glove total was tops for a third baseman and the most for any position.

It was also a successful year for the future Hall of Famer at the plate. Robinson reached career highs nearly across the board. He led the league in runs batted in (118) and had more extra-base hits (66) than strikeouts (64).

"Is Brooks the best ever at third?" asked Hall of Fame third baseman George Kell, a teammate of Robinson's in 1957. "No doubt about it."

## JOHNNY BENCH  1970, 1972 (NL)

BEHIND THE PLATE, CINCINNATI REDS CATCHER Johnny Bench took a beating. "Go out and get hit by a car every four or five days," is how Bench described being a catcher.

The physical toll of being an everyday catcher made the fact that Bench was able to swing such a powerful bat even more impressive. The National League MVP in 1970 and 1972 hit 85 homers in those two seasons and drove in a combined 273 runs.

Bench also had a cannon for an arm. And he knew it. At age 22 he boasted he could "throw out any runner alive." And it was certainly hard to see why baserunners would challenge him. In 1970 he threw out 48 percent of runners attempting to steal. And in 1972, he caught 56 percent.

When he hung up his shin guards after the 1983 season, Bench was considered by many to be both the finest offensive *and* defensive catcher in history.

"Is he the greatest catcher who ever caught?" Sparky Anderson, his manager in Cincinnati for nine years, wondered a few years after Bench had finished his playing career. "This man is in a class of his own."

### AVERAGE TOTALS FOR MVP SEASONS

| HR | RBI | AVG | FP |
|----|-----|-----|-----|
| 43 | 137 | .282 | .989 |

| HR | RBI | AVG | FP |
|----|-----|------|------|
| 6 | 63 | .267 | .972 |

## MARTY MARION  1944 (NL)

MARTY MARION WAS NO SLOUCH AT THE PLATE. But it is a great testament to his defense that no one has ever won an MVP Award with a lower batting average than his .267 mark in 1944. His teammate in St. Louis, Hall of Famer Stan Musial, hit .347 that year and Chicago's Bill Nicholson hit 33 homers, but the honor went to Marion, who was unsurpassed as a shortstop.

Musial saw firsthand how much ground Marion could cover and how he could rifle a throw. "The thing about it was, he had such a great arm and his ball was as light as a feather," Musial said. "And extremely accurate … he had the most accurate arm you ever saw. The ball was always right there."

With an offense featuring Musial, Johnny Hopp and Walker Cooper, Marion in the field, and an ace in righty Mort Cooper (the '42 MVP), the Cardinals won the World Series in 1944 (the franchise won it in 1942 and '46, as well).

That's not to say that Marion was ineffective as a hitter that season. Far from it, in fact. He had 26 doubles in 1944 and 63 RBI. But Marion, once nicknamed "The Octopus" for his reach at short, won the MVP Award for his defense. "Nobody's ever played shortstop as well as I did," Marion said years after his retirement. Then he said with a laugh: "And I didn't lack for confidence, either."

# chapter 4
# WINNERS

*Since the MVP Award took on its modern form in 1931, eight Major League pitchers with 25 or more wins in a season have claimed the honor. Seven of them — the exception being Hal Newhouser of the 1944 Detroit Tigers — reached the World Series. It's true that in addition to great stuff, these star hurlers had great supporting casts; otherwise they would not have reached such lofty win totals or gotten to the Fall Classic. But more so, they had workhorse attitudes on the mound. Six threw 300 innings or more. Seven worked 20 or more complete games. As the saying goes, you have to be in it to win it.*

## SANDY KOUFAX 1963 (NL)

THE LAST BATTER TO FACE SANDY KOUFAX ON MAY 11, 1963, WAS Harvey Kuenn, the Giants' left fielder and leadoff man. A career .303 hitter, Kuenn managed just a dribbler back to the mound, which the legendary Koufax quickly gobbled up and tossed to first to seal his second career no-hitter.

Koufax, the left-handed ace (and cult hero) of the Los Angeles Dodgers, was special that evening, shutting down the rival Giants. Of course, he was special throughout the 1963 season, winning the NL MVP Award and his first Cy Young Award.

The 1963 Dodgers won 99 games and the World Series, thanks in part to their pitching — the best in the Majors at the time. Koufax and Don Drysdale were the Hall of Fame front-liners. They won 25 and 19 games, respectively. "I can see how he won 25 games," Yogi Berra later said of Koufax. "What I don't understand is how he lost five."

With his lethal, triple-digit fastball, Koufax was a bit wild in his early days. It was enough to raise doubts when the Dodgers signed the Brooklyn native in the mid-1950s. At Spring Training in 1955, famed sportswriter Red Smith took note, watching a nervous Koufax sail one of his big fastballs over the catcher's head. But any question marks were a distant memory by 1963. By then, Koufax's pitches were completely under control — and totally unhittable.

He struck out 306 that year, including four Giants during his May 11 no-hitter, and posted a staggering 1.88 ERA. He would twirl four no-hitters in his career, one per year from 1962 to 1965 (including a perfect game in '65). Koufax went 111-34 from 1962 to 1966, probably the most dominant stretch by any pitcher in history. All of those victories added up to three pennants and two World Series crowns for the Dodgers.

| W | L | ERA | IP |
|----|---|------|-----|
| 25 | 5 | 1.88 | 311 |

| W | L | ERA | IP |
|----|---|------|-------|
| 30 | 7 | 2.66 | 311.7 |

## DIZZY DEAN 1934 (NL)

IN LOUD FASHION, THE 1934 ST. LOUIS CARDINALS, FONDLY REFERRED to as the Gas House Gang, won 95 games and the World Series. Known as much for their off-field antics as for their on-field dominance, the Cardinals featured the brothers Dean (Dizzy and Paul) at the top of their rotation. While Paul, who went 19-11, was soft-spoken, his older brother Dizzy attracted attention both for his remarkable right arm and his fondness for colorful storytelling.

Dizzy's numbers in 1934 told quite a tale. He went 30-7 and led the league in Ks with 195. It was an MVP effort for sure, and the signature year of his Hall of Fame career. But even on days when he was not the featured story, the Arkansas native found a way to get his name into print.

Case in point: The Deans dominated a doubleheader against the Brooklyn Dodgers on Sept. 21. Dizzy threw a three-hit shutout in Game 1, but was outdone by Paul, who threw a no-hitter in Game 2. "I didn't know in that first game that nobody had a hit offa me until the eighth inning," Dizzy said, in his famous English-ish way. "I shoulda knowed, then I coulda really breezed them in there, and we'd both had us a no-hitter."

Although foot and arm injuries cut Dizzy's career short, he was ushered into Cooperstown soon after his retirement. Not one to fade into the background, Dean soon got behind a microphone, where he charmed baseball fans for 20-plus years as a broadcaster. "He would say a player 'slud into third' as another 'threwed' the ball," Jim Etter later recalled in *The Daily Oklahoman*, "and that a good batter could be 'mighty hitterish.'"

Dizzy also won two games in the 1934 World Series against Detroit, including an 11-0 shutout in Game 7.

HUBBELL'S
SPIKES

| W | L | ERA | IP |
|---|---|-----|-----|
| 26 | 6 | 2.31 | 304 |

## CARL HUBBELL 1936 (NL)

IN A SPORT SO OBSESSED WITH STREAKS, CARL HUBBELL'S RUN OF WINS has often been overlooked. It began on July 17, 1936, when the southpaw led the New York Giants to a 6-0 victory over the Pirates at Pittsburgh's Forbes Field. He would win his next 15 decisions in 1936, earning his second MVP nod (his first was in 1933) and helping the Giants roll to the NL pennant.

The key to Hubbell's success was a lethal screwball — a pitch he threw over the top like a fastball — that would tail fiercely away from right-handed batters. "Hitters always have one thing in mind: They have to protect themselves against the fastball," Hubbell once said. "If they're ready for the fastball and don't get it, they can adjust to the breaking ball. But with a screwball, it isn't the break that fools the hitter, it's the change of speed. They don't time it."

Hubbell developed his famous pitch out of necessity. Playing in the Western League, he couldn't get right-handed hitters out because his off-speed stuff seemed to sail right into their sweet spots. "They were killing me," he lamented. The screwball, which he claimed to have learned from teammate Lefty Thomas, gave Hubbell some much-needed help.

He would win 26 games in 1936, the highest tally in the Bigs. He also led all hurlers in ERA (2.31) and WHIP (1.059). Although his Giants lost the '36 Series to the Yankees, Hubbell won Game 1, holding Lou Gehrig, Joe DiMaggio and the rest of the crosstown rivals to just one run on seven hits. Eight wins in a row at the start of the 1937 campaign brought his streak of consecutive regular-season victories to 24. He retired after the 1943 season and was enshrined in Cooperstown with the game's elite soon after.

Hubbell (pitching)

WINNERS

| W | L | ERA | IP |
|---|---|-----|-----|
| 27 | 7 | 3.06 | 268 |

## DON NEWCOMBE
## 1956 (NL)

THE SECOND HALF OF PITCHER Don Newcombe's 1956 campaign wasn't as good as Carl Hubbell's had been 20 years prior. The Dodgers' imposing righty did actually lose games during August and September. Well, one game in each month, in an 18-2 run to end a 27-7 season. It wasn't exactly a tailspin.

Newcombe pitched with impeccable control that entire season, walking just 46 batters. Take his Sept. 19 start against St. Louis, when he allowed two runs in seven innings and walked none, for win No. 25. No slouch at the plate, either, "Newk" went 3 for 4 that day with two homers.

For his 1956 efforts, Newcombe earned the first-ever Cy Young Award (given to the best Big League pitcher, rather than the best from each league) and the NL MVP Award. Despite winning a World Series title the previous year, he called winning both trophies that year his "proudest achievement." Having been Rookie of the Year in 1949, he became the first to take all three honors.

It's hard to measure his social impact, but Newcombe's success — along with his other African-American teammates — with the Dodgers was noted by civil rights activists. "Martin Luther King sat down at my dinner table and told me how we made his job easier," Newcombe said, recalling a conversation in 1968, one month before King's assassination. "He was being beat up by sticks, and he said we made things easier for him."

## BUCKY WALTERS 1939 (NL)

OF BUCKY WALTERS' 27 WINS IN 1939, THE MOST HISTORIC CAME on Aug. 26, when he carried the Cincinnati Reds past the Brooklyn Dodgers at Ebbets Field, 5-2. That Walters won was nothing new; the Reds ace won nearly 70 percent of his 39 appearances that year. But for the first time ever, people outside the park watched the victory, as NBC made it baseball's first televised affair.

Much of his 1939 on-field performance was TV-worthy, as he won the pitching Triple Crown — leading the NL in wins, ERA (2.29) and strikeouts (137). He also hit .325 in 120 at-bats, knocking in 16 runs.

Walters moved to the mound at the behest of Phillies Manager Jimmie Wilson in 1934. He was

| W | L | ERA | IP |
|---|---|---|---|
| 27 | 11 | 2.29 | 319 |

traded to the Reds in 1938, where he used his dangerous sinking fastball and slider to devastate hitters. With Walters and righty Paul Derringer, the Reds had a frightful pitching duo. Derringer went 25-7 for the '39 Reds, who won 97 games and went on to the World Series (where they fell to Joe DiMaggio and the Yankees).

The modest Walters truly loved competing, leaving him with just one regret about the move to pitcher: "I just wish I could have played every day," he later said.

McLAIN'S GLOVE

### DENNY McLAIN 1968 (AL)

EITHER ON TOP OF THE WORLD OR AT rock bottom, Denny McLain never seemed to spend much time in between. The Tigers' ace peaked in 1968, speeding to 31 wins, countless standing ovations and the AL MVP and Cy Young awards.

McLain brought a vicious fastball and an in-your-face style to the hill. "I throw the pitch I want," he told *Life* in 1968, "and make them try to hit it."

McLain made 41 starts that season. He had an 8-1 record by the end of May, capping the month with a complete-game, 13-K shutout against the California Angels. He finished with 280 strikeouts and a 1.96 ERA on the season for the Tigers (who would defeat the Cardinals in the World Series). All

despite an arm injury midway through the year, that necessitated a shot of cortisone before every start.

He also declined to ease up off the field. "I was anywhere and everywhere," he wrote in his autobiography, *Strikeout*. "Go to a shopping center and you'd see me behind the keyboard of a Hammond organ. Turn on your TV and you'd see me on everything from the *Today Show* to *Joey Bishop*. The only thing I wasn't doing much was sleeping."

His non-stop lifestyle caught up with him when a shoulder injury forced McLain out of the game in 1972. And his turbulent life and legal trouble after baseball featured at least as many highs and lows, if not more. Few fans, though, will forget the righty's '68 campaign.

**SAME YEAR CY YOUNG AWARD & MVP WINNERS**

| PLAYER | TEAM | YEAR |
| --- | --- | --- |
| Sandy Koufax | Los Angeles Dodgers | 1963 |
| Bob Gibson | St. Louis Cardinals | 1968 |
| Denny McLain | Detroit Tigers | 1968 |
| Vida Blue | Oakland Athletics | 1971 |
| Rollie Fingers | Milwaukee Brewers | 1981 |
| Willie Hernandez | Detroit Tigers | 1984 |
| Roger Clemens | Boston Red Sox | 1986 |
| Dennis Eckersley | Oakland Athletics | 1992 |
| Justin Verlander | Detroit Tigers | 2011 |

## LEFTY GROVE  1931 (AL)

THEY CALLED HIM LEFTY, AND FOR GOOD REASON — HALL OF FAME hurler Robert Moses Grove truly was one of the finest southpaws in history.

The feather in his cap was the 1931 season, when he won the AL MVP Award (in the first year of its modern form). That season, Grove won 31 games, losing just four, in 30 starts and just 41 appearances for the Philadelphia Athletics. He also won the pitching Triple Crown, adding a 2.06 ERA, 175 Ks and four saves to his impressive win total.

Similar to many other MVP-winning hurlers, Grove was notorious for his competitive fire on the hill. After reeling off 16 straight victories in 1931, he lost a 1-0 decision to the St. Louis Browns. On a key play during that game, Jim Moore, a rookie A's outfielder playing in place of Hall of Famer Al Simmons, misplayed a fly ball. In the locker room, Grove allegedly went ballistic, knocking down lockers and destroying

| W | L | ERA | IP |
|----|----|------|-------|
| 31 | 4 | 2.06 | 288.7 |

his own uniform. "If Simmons had been here and in left field," Grove insisted, "he would have caught that ball in his back pocket." For years, he held Simmons responsible for the end of his win streak.

Upon his death in 1975, Grove left his MVP Award trophy to his hometown of Lonaconing, Md., a coal-mining community in the western part of the state. The Groves were a mining family, and Lefty never forgot his roots. Having put the trophy on display in the local library in 2001, it's clear the town won't soon forget Grove's 1931 heroics, either.

Grove started three games against the St. Louis Cardinals in the 1931 World Series. He went 2-1 with a 2.42 ERA.

# chapter 5
# HITTING MACHINES

*Some were historically patient. Others, notoriously impatient. And while some could clear the outfield wall almost at will, others rarely tried. Each of these big-hitting MVPs brought a hitting talent to the plate that was flat-out dominant. They reached base — be it by home run, by line drive or by infield hit — day in and day out. Cincinnati's Ernie Lombardi is one of them; the 1938 MVP won a batting title with a .342 average and just 14 strikeouts. So is Dick Groat, who rapped 186 hits in 573 at-bats for the Pirates in his award-winning 1960 season. They're in good company.*

## JOE DiMAGGIO  1941 (AL)

IT BEGAN QUIETLY — A FIRST-INNING SINGLE OFF CHICAGO'S EDDIE Smith on May 15 — but each day it continued. New York's Joe DiMaggio piled up the hits in 1941, eventually reaching a remarkable all-time-record 56-game hit streak, and ultimately claiming the AL MVP Award.

DiMaggio himself became aware of the run at 19 games, after he had two hits against Cleveland's Bob Feller on June 22. "But I didn't think too much about it," he said. The Yankee Clipper rapped a single off Detroit's Dizzy Trout on June 24, to set the team record at 34.

DiMaggio was known to be, like many ballplayers, a bit superstitious. His hand had been bandaged during the first game of a 61-game hit streak in the Minors, so he had to have it taped before every contest of that run for fear of messing with his luck. Similarly, DiMaggio always stepped on second base on his way to the outfield. So he was alarmed to learn, between games of a double-header (Nos. 41 and 42 of "The Streak"), that his bat had been stolen. As word spread, his teammates grew worried, too. "It was just a piece of wood," DiMaggio said, "but the bench was like a funeral parlor." Teammate Tommy Henrich heroically swooped in, returning an old bat that DiMaggio had lent him, and the magical streak continued.

It finally came to a halt on July 17, thanks in part to a pair of remarkable plays by Indians' third baseman Ken Keltner. During the historic stretch, DiMaggio hit .408 (91 for 223), blasted 15 home runs and knocked in 55 runs. But the true greatness he displayed over the course of the streak was hard to quantify. "Baseball isn't statistics," writer Jimmy Breslin once said. "It's Joe DiMaggio rounding second base."

| HR | RBI | AVG | HITS | OBP |
|----|-----|-----|------|-----|
| 30 | 125 | .357 | 193 | .440 |

## GEORGE BRETT 1980 (AL)

ALL EYES WERE ON GEORGE BRETT IN 1980. THEY WATCHED AS HE walked to the batting cage to loosen up, sat rapt when he stepped into the box to smack another line drive, and crowded by his locker after games. The Kansas City Royals' third baseman was on fire, flirting with a .400 average during an MVP season — and no one wanted to miss a second.

Reporters followed Brett everywhere, seeking comment on his remarkable campaign. "I've never been this hot this long," he marveled in August. "I'm just going to try to keep telling myself that I'm hot. The thing I don't want to do is put pressure on myself. But it's hard not to think about what I'm hitting."

The game's other stars took notice, too. Before a game at Yankee Stadium in mid-July, New York slugger Reggie Jackson paused to watch a bit of Royals batting practice. "Just wanna watch Brett. I've never seen a man hitting .570," Jackson exaggerated. Brett went 7 for 14 during the three-game set, raising his actual average to .375.

| HR | RBI | AVG | HITS | OBP |
|----|-----|------|------|------|
| 24 | 118 | .390 | 175 | .454 |

One particular at-bat during the 1980 season even caught the eye of a farm animal. As Brett approached the plate in Cleveland, a chicken mascot bowed toward the plate. As he got ready in the box, the chicken bit its nails. And when he ripped a stand-up double, the chicken clapped politely, shaking its head in disbelief.

Brett just missed .400 (.390) that year, which hardly diminished his season. He had hit well over .400 in June, July and August, striking out in just 22 of 449 at-bats. Said Yankees hitting coach Charlie Lau: "The only one who can get George out is George."

# Brett hit .375 (9 for 24) in the World Series, but the Royals lost to Philly in six games.

## ROD CAREW 1977 (AL)

AT THE PLATE, ROD CAREW RELIED ON HIS WRISTS. The bat lay nearly horizontal in Carew's hands, his arms moving it back and forth as the pitcher went into his windup. At just the right moment, those wrists would whip the bat through the zone, directing the ball, it seemed, anywhere he wanted. "Rodney is not mechanically perfect," said Carew's manager in Minnesota, Gene Mauch. "But he doesn't have to be. He has his own way."

Carew's way certainly worked for him. A seven-time batting champ, he had perhaps his finest season in 1977, when he set career highs nearly across the board, in average (.388), hits (239) and RBI (100). He would easily win the AL MVP Award.

The future Hall of Famer swung a 34-inch, 32-ounce piece of lumber that year and was known to lift 20-pound dumbbells to get his wrists ready for action.

| HR | RBI | AVG | HITS | OBP |
|----|-----|-----|------|-----|
| 14 | 100 | .388 | 239 | .449 |

JEFF BAGWELL **1994 (NL)**

IN 1994, THREE YEARS AFTER WINNING THE ROOKIE of the Year Award, Houston's Jeff Bagwell reached a new level. "I don't think I can play much better," Bagwell said after his MVP-winning season. "I'm almost worried about if I can do it again."

In a season shortened by a players' strike, Bagwell made the most of 400 at-bats, hitting .368 with 39 homers (setting a club record with 23 at the Astrodome), 32 doubles and 116 RBI. He was the fourth-ever unanimous choice for MVP in league history (along with Carl Hubbell, Orlando Cepeda and Mike Schmidt).

But the public support didn't come as a result of any self-promotion. Teammates spoke of him as a quiet competitor

| HR | RBI | AVG | HITS | OBP |
|----|-----|-----|------|-----|
| 39 | 116 | .368 | 147 | .451 |

who let his performance do the talking. Bagwell, they said, deflected most personal praise to the team. Still, said Houston second baseman Craig Biggio, "What people don't realize is how hard the guy works."

Bagwell didn't go more than 10 at-bats in 1994 without a hit, and his average never dropped below .323. "The one thing about MVP seasons that stands out is consistency," teammate Doug Drabek said. "To me, that was the most impressive thing about his season. It just seemed like he never hit a bad spot or had a period where he wasn't just crushing the ball."

On June 26, Carew entered a game against the White Sox batting .396. Two hits later, the scoreboard read: "Rod Carew is batting .400!" Going 4 for 5, he pushed his average to .403.

"That whole month … it was the most amazing thing I've ever seen from a hitter," teammate Roy Smalley recalled. "He wasn't hitting a bunch of little flares to left. It seemed like he was hitting every pitch on the fat part of the bat."

MUSIAL'S
JERSEY

| HR | RBI | AVG | HITS | OBP |
|----|-----|-----|------|-----|
| 39 | 131 | .376 | 230 | .450 |

## STAN MUSIAL 1948 (NL)

STAN MUSIAL WAS A TRUE GENTLEMAN, BUT he could be lethal with a bat. From his coiled stance, the lifetime Cardinal unleashed all of his might on the ball with each and every swing, collecting seven batting titles and three MVP Awards. He hit .357 in his 1943 MVP effort and .365 to win again in 1946.

Then came 1948, his third MVP season, widely considered to be his finest. A career .331 batter, Musial hit .376 that year. But it wasn't just the jump in average that made 1948 special. It was how productive his hits were. He stroked 39 homers, 20 more than he ever had before, and drove in a career-high 131.

It was no coincidence. Growing up in Donora, Pa., the lefty idolized Pirates outfielder Paul Waner — a .333-hitter with little power. "I wanted to be a .300 hitter, too," Musial said, "so I started out punching the ball to left." But that changed in 1948 when Musial, having watched the likes of Ralph Kiner and Johnny Mize slug their way to fame, decided to go deep. He got a lighter bat and started to pull the ball.

But even more remarkable than the jump in power was how unaffected Musial's overall success was by the new approach. He struck out just 34 times in 1948, only three more than he had in his 1946 MVP effort, and hit at a career-high clip.

When asked how one was supposed to get Musial out, Brooklyn's Preacher Roe said it best: "I throw him four wide ones, then try to pick him off first base."

## ICHIRO SUZUKI
## 2001 (AL)

ICHIRO SUZUKI, AMONG JAPAN'S most popular baseball stars and a wizard of a contact hitter, landed in the Bigs in 2001. He went opposite field for Seattle. He drove it up the middle. He even pulled homers. The slim outfielder seemed capable of anything at the plate — except whiffing. And with blazing speed and a quick jump off contact, he seemed to zoom through first before the ball even reached a defender.

"I don't think you can pitch him one way," then Yankees Manager Joe Torre said in Ichiro's rookie year. "He makes the adjustment. You can get ahead in the count and he still seems relaxed. He doesn't seem to have any weaknesses."

Hitting .336 in his first 25 games, and .379 in May, players raved, Japanese media swarmed and Ichiro took it in stride. "I think he probably surprised everyone but himself," said teammate David Bell.

For Bell, the most impressive at-bat that year came against White Sox reliever Kelly Wunsch. Bell recalled that Ichiro appeared overmatched on the first two pitches. "Then all of a sudden, he fouls a few balls off, and you have no idea how he makes contact," Bell said. "Before you know it, he hits a ground ball up the middle."

Ichiro hit .318 in 2001 against lefties with a .350 overall clip, and led the league in plate appearances (738) and hits (242) to take his first batting title. With a stellar throwing arm, Ichiro also took the Rookie of the Year title and his first Gold Glove in right field — the icing on an MVP debut.

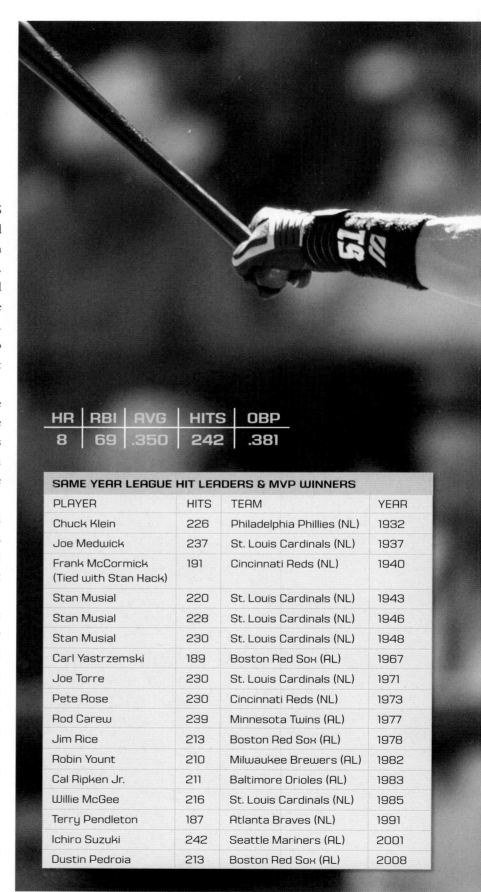

| HR | RBI | AVG | HITS | OBP |
|---|---|---|---|---|
| 8 | 69 | .350 | 242 | .381 |

### SAME YEAR LEAGUE HIT LEADERS & MVP WINNERS

| PLAYER | HITS | TEAM | YEAR |
|---|---|---|---|
| Chuck Klein | 226 | Philadelphia Phillies (NL) | 1932 |
| Joe Medwick | 237 | St. Louis Cardinals (NL) | 1937 |
| Frank McCormick (Tied with Stan Hack) | 191 | Cincinnati Reds (NL) | 1940 |
| Stan Musial | 220 | St. Louis Cardinals (NL) | 1943 |
| Stan Musial | 228 | St. Louis Cardinals (NL) | 1946 |
| Stan Musial | 230 | St. Louis Cardinals (NL) | 1948 |
| Carl Yastrzemski | 189 | Boston Red Sox (AL) | 1967 |
| Joe Torre | 230 | St. Louis Cardinals (NL) | 1971 |
| Pete Rose | 230 | Cincinnati Reds (NL) | 1973 |
| Rod Carew | 239 | Minnesota Twins (AL) | 1977 |
| Jim Rice | 213 | Boston Red Sox (AL) | 1978 |
| Robin Yount | 210 | Milwaukee Brewers (AL) | 1982 |
| Cal Ripken Jr. | 211 | Baltimore Orioles (AL) | 1983 |
| Willie McGee | 216 | St. Louis Cardinals (NL) | 1985 |
| Terry Pendleton | 187 | Atlanta Braves (NL) | 1991 |
| Ichiro Suzuki | 242 | Seattle Mariners (AL) | 2001 |
| Dustin Pedroia | 213 | Boston Red Sox (AL) | 2008 |

| HR | RBI | AVG | HITS | OBP |
|----|-----|-----|------|-----|
| 29 | 114 | .331 | 210 | .379 |

## ROBIN YOUNT  1982 (AL)

BREWERS STAR SHORTSTOP AND 1982 AL MVP ROBIN Yount was popular with his home crowd from the moment of his Big League debut at age 18 in 1974. Although he was already a gifted and passionate all-around player, he used his early at-bats to weather the ups and downs of the Majors. "Hitting was tough for me," he admitted, "because the pitchers were so much more experienced than I was. But if you take what they give you, and learn to adjust when you get into a slump, you can hit them."

He hit them consistently in 1982, collecting league-leading totals but keeping his mind in touch with the humbled teenager of years before. He was once asked how he avoided being egotistical.

"What's that mean?" he replied. A swelled head, was the answer. "Nah," he said, reading the tag in his hat. "It's 6 7/8."

"I'm just a human being gifted with the ability to play baseball," he said. "I'm nothing special. I'm just another person."

Yount fell a percentage point short of the batting title (.331, to Willie Wilson's .332) in 1982, but there was no doubt he was the best in the AL that year. Yount hit .341 with six homers in the season's final two months, ensuring Milwaukee a postseason spot. In the last weeks, home fans offered prophetic chants of "MVP!" "He's uncomfortable with that chant," said teammate Ted Simmons. "You can see his jaw kind of clench."

| HR | RBI | AVG | HITS | OBP |
|----|-----|-----|------|-----|
| 18 | 106 | .355 | 199 | .453 |

## LOU BOUDREAU
# 1948 (AL)

LOOKING BACK, INDIANS OWNER Bill Veeck must have been relieved that he kept Lou Boudreau for the 1948 season. When fans got word of a plan to send Cleveland's shortstop-manager to St. Louis, they let the owner have it. But the deal fell through. "I have heard you," Veeck responded. "Lou won't be traded."

Boudreau, clearly a star on the field, had taken over as player-manager in 1942 at age 24. While his skills at the plate and glove work were unquestionable, he had yet to prove he could guide the team after his first six seasons as skipper.

But Boudreau did it in 1948, after the idea of trading him was squashed. With his bat, glove and leadership, he steered the Tribe to a World Series title, grabbing some individual hardware on the way. Boudreau hit a career-high .355 that season, while walking 98 times with just nine strikeouts. Cleveland finished the regular season tied with Boston, resulting in a one-game playoff in which Boudreau went 4 for 4 with two homers. "In 1948," Veeck later wrote, "Lou had the greatest season any player has ever had."

Although he was young and well liked, Boudreau was no pushover as a manager. He was known to find out which players were breaking the 12 a.m. curfew by giving a baseball to the elevator operator who started his shift at midnight, and telling him to get some autographs. Said Arne Harris, Boudreau's friend: "The next day he'd ask, 'Let's see who signed your ball.'"

## PETE ROSE  1973 (NL)

RAISED IN CINCINNATI, PETE ROSE WAS NO PHYSICAL SPECIMEN. He had neither the frame nor the natural grace to suggest he'd one day win an NL MVP Award, let alone become the game's all-time hits leader (he passed Ty Cobb in 1985 and finished his career with 4,256 hits). Big League scouts never flocked to see him. "But Pete just decided he was going to make himself into a great player, and did," said Eddie Brinkman, a childhood friend.

They came to call Rose Charlie Hustle, because like his idol growing up, Enos Slaughter, Rose had a motor that wouldn't quit. In 1973, the switch-hitting outfielder scratched and clawed his way to 230 hits, a personal best in a 24-year career with 10 200-hit seasons. His .338 average that year was tops in the NL.

Batting leadoff, Rose set the tone for a great offense (Cincinnati finished second in the league in runs scored). The 1973 West Division champs topped Walter Alston's Dodgers by 3.5 games, as Rose got himself on base for middle-of-the-order sluggers like Johnny Bench and Tony Perez. He scored 115 runs with a .401 OBP.

The Reds, then nicknamed "The Big Red Machine," dominated for much of the decade, and won the World Series in 1975 and '76. In Game 3 of his team's NLCS showdown against the Mets in 1973, Rose slid hard into shortstop Bud Harrelson and came up brawling. It would be perhaps the lasting memory of his MVP season — further evidence that Rose played with a fire like few others. "I just try to play hard every day," he said.

| HR | RBI | AVG | HITS | OBP |
|----|-----|------|------|------|
| 5 | 64 | .338 | 230 | .401 |

Gehringer (swinging)

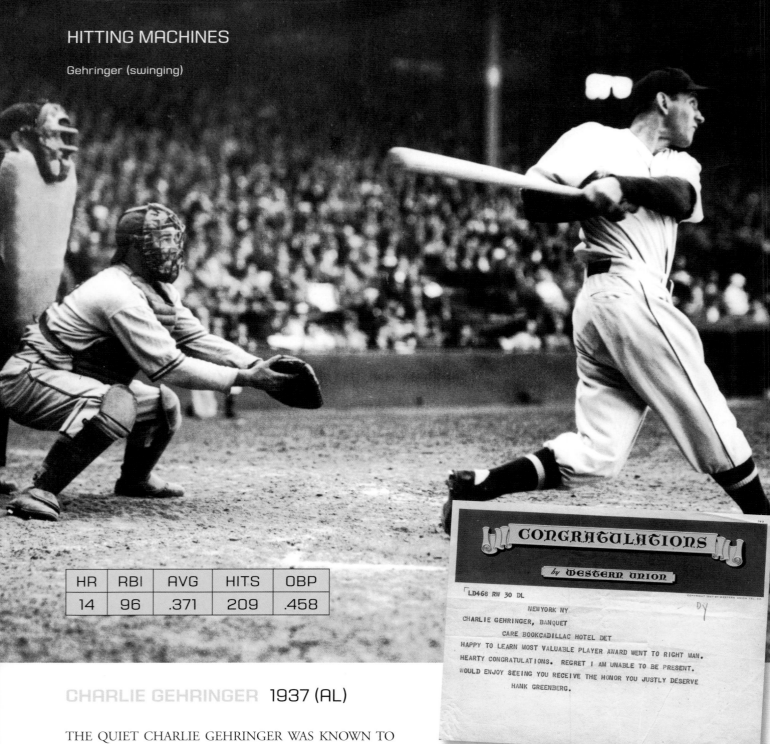

| HR | RBI | AVG | HITS | OBP |
|----|-----|-----|------|-----|
| 14 | 96 | .371 | 209 | .458 |

CONGRATULATIONS
by WESTERN UNION

LD468 RW 30 DL

NEWYORK NY
CHARLIE GEHRINGER, BANQUET
CARE BOOKCADILLAC HOTEL DET
HAPPY TO LEARN MOST VALUABLE PLAYER AWARD WENT TO RIGHT MAN.
HEARTY CONGRATULATIONS. REGRET I AM UNABLE TO BE PRESENT.
WOULD ENJOY SEEING YOU RECEIVE THE HONOR YOU JUSTLY DESERVE
HANK GREENBERG.

## CHARLIE GEHRINGER   1937 (AL)

THE QUIET CHARLIE GEHRINGER WAS KNOWN TO many as "The Mechanical Man." But what he lacked in vocal leadership, the Tigers second baseman more than made up for with physical ability. A wildly consistent player, Gehringer reached a career-high average (.371) in 1937 to win the AL MVP Award.

He entered 1937 on a string of four straight 200-hit seasons. In 1934, Gehringer had finished behind Lou Gehrig in the AL batting race (.356) and second in the MVP vote.

But 1937 was Gehringer's year. His average was tops in the league, 20 points clear of Gehrig's. He scored 133 runs and struck out just 25 times. Gehringer was a natural in the field, too, gliding into the hole to take away a hit or turn a double play. He made just 12 errors that year in 142 games. While the Tigers finished 13 games behind the Yankees in the 1937 standings, the MVP voters placed Detroit's star first.

Those who saw Gehringer play describe a natural grace; at the plate, the ball seemed to jump off of his bat. Although he comfortably passed the .300 mark almost annually, he could have hit much higher: Fellow Hall of Famer Bucky Harris once declared that "year after year he leads the league in hot line drives right at someone."

## DAVE PARKER  1978 (NL)

TO ANGER DAVE PARKER, PITTSBURGH'S STAR OF the 1970s and early '80s, was an error in judgment. But someone tried it in Philadelphia in September 1978, calling in a death threat to the 6-foot-5 outfielder. Afterward, Parker turned up his MVP game, hitting .500 in the next eight games and helping the Bucs cut two games off the Phillies' four-game division lead.

Throughout his career, Parker was an aggressive competitor, one who would run through a catcher even in a sandlot game. "I love to run over people," he crowed. He was a spectacular talent,

winning back-to-back batting titles in 1977 and '78 and the MVP Award for his work during the latter season.

He did everything for the Pirates that year, hitting .334 and leading the team with 30 homers and 117 RBI. Parker also won a Gold Glove in the outfield.

Parker hit .412 in September and October that year, lighting up the Cubs on Sept. 19 with a 4-for-6, two-home run day.

"I'm the foundation," Parker said with trademark confidence that season. "They build around me." And although the Pirates came up short to Philadelphia, MVP voters seemed to concur.

| HR | RBI | AVG | HITS | OBP |
|----|-----|------|------|------|
| 30 | 117 | .334 | 194 | .394 |

## VLADIMIR GUERRERO 2004 (AL)

MANY WORDS CAN DESCRIBE VLADIMIR GUERRERO: Powerful, talented and aggressive are all options. But patient is not. "If [the ball]'s coming forward," Vlad's teammate John Lackey told *The Orange County Register* in 2004, "he's pretty much going to swing at it." And whether the ball scrapes the dirt or flies up by his eyes, inside or way out, odds are Guerrero is going to drive it.

He certainly did in 2004, swinging the Angels to an AL West title. Guerrero, a Dominican Republic native, was particularly fearsome down the stretch, posting a .363 clip with 11 longballs and 25 RBI in his last 30 games. That run, many in the media speculated, pushed him over the top in the MVP chase.

In one four-game set in Texas during the final week of the year, Guerrero hit five homers and knocked in nine. The Angels

won three, moving from one game behind the A's to a tie for first place (they would win the division by one game). "Not many players can do what he did," Manager Mike Scioscia said. "To almost single-handedly carry us to the pennant, it was incredible."

Guerrero hit 39 home runs on his way to an American League-best 366 total bases. He also finished third in the league in average (.337).

The heroics came in Guerrero's first season in the sun, having signed the winter prior with the Angels as a free agent after eight years in Montreal. Despite whispers about Guerrero's supposedly bad back, the right fielder played 156 games for Anaheim, including 143 in the outfield. "When he came to our team," Scioscia said after the MVP winner was announced, "our expectations obviously were very high, and he met every one of them."

| HR | RBI | AVG | HITS | OBP |
|----|-----|-----|------|-----|
| 24 | 137 | .363 | 230 | .421 |

## JOE TORRE  1971 (NL)

JOE TORRE, THE MANAGER, HAS had a good number of memorable baseball seasons. His near handful of World Series rings is proof of that. Joe Torre, the player, had a pretty special career as well. Within it, 1971 stands out. "Even now, I'm pretty impressed with the numbers," he said 20 years after his 1971 MVP season. "I think the consistency is the thing I'm most proud of."

Consistency indeed. Torre, who would go on to win the batting title that year by posting a .363 average, never hit lower than .324 during any given month of that season. Out of 161 games played, the St. Louis Cardinal went hitless in just 28 instances. "I was just so tuned in to what I was doing," he said.

Having started his playing career as a catcher, it might have helped that Torre was a full-fledged third baseman by the beginning of that season. "Catching gets you in the legs and the back," he said, "and that affects everything else."

Thanks to his position change, he felt strong as the clean-up hitter for St. Louis in 1971, and it showed. He led the league in hits (230) and RBI (137) and come award time, left Hall of Famers like Willie Stargell, Hank Aaron and Roberto Clemente in his MVP dust. "You will see some players who have a hot streak," teammate Dal Maxvill said, "where maybe they hit .360 and get a lot of RBI. They are picture-perfect for a while, but it's just a matter of time before they wear out. That year, from day one, Joe was hot."

| HR | RBI | AVG | HITS | OBP |
|----|-----|-----|------|-----|
| 49 | 130 | .366 | 208 | .452 |

## LARRY WALKER  1997 (NL)

THE ARMCHAIR CRITIC IN MOST WOULD GREET IT with a natural skepticism — a Rockies player for MVP? Surely his numbers were inflated by the hitter-friendly air of Denver. But just a 30-second examination of Larry Walker's 1997 stats silences the debate. He did hit .384 at home with 20 home runs. But the star right fielder also was consistently successful elsewhere — hitting .346 and belting 29 longballs away from Coors Field. "I don't care where you play," teammate Ellis Burks said during the season, "you can't diminish the man's numbers."

The 1997 Rockies kicked off the season on the road. And in the second series, a three-game set in Montreal, Walker went 7 for 13 with four homers and seven RBI. A later series in Pittsburgh yielded similar results (10 for 16, four homers, six RBI).

All that production brought hardware to Denver at season's end. Walker finished second in the batting race, his .366 clip just a few points behind Tony Gwynn's .372. He also had led the league in total bases (409) and OPS (1.172), to go with a healthy 33 steals, 130 RBI and his third Gold Glove.

Writers flocked to Walker that season, as they tend to do when a slugger rakes with such consistency. But he took it in stride. Wrote Jim Murray in the *Los Angeles Times*: "I've known designated hitters who were haughtier."

Mantle struck out just 75 times in '57,
a personal best for a season in which
he played 100 or more games.

MICKEY MANTLE    1957 (AL)

IN 1957, SWITCH-HITTING YANKEES LEGEND MICKEY MANTLE LOST A
historic batting race to Red Sox great Ted Williams, .388 to .365. Had he kept up his
torrent August pace, Mantle may have had a chance. After going 3 for 7 in a double-
header against the Orioles on Aug. 18, the Yankees center fielder trailed Williams .392 to
.385. But Williams was too good. "I loved watching Ted hit," Mantle confessed.

But most any baseball fan loved watching Mantle hit, too. And although he came up
short in the race for the batting crown, Mantle's historic 1957 season still garnered the
AL MVP Award at season's end, his second straight (he would add a third in 1962).

Were the voters mistaken to reward Mantle and not Boston's Splendid Splinter?
Noted baseball writer and statistician Bill James doesn't think so. "For my part as a
statistical analyst," James once wrote, "I would like to say that anyone who thinks Ted
Williams in 1957 was a better player than Mickey Mantle is a lunatic." Mantle, he ar-
gued, was far more valuable defensively that season, and quicker on the bases. He also
drove in and scored more runs and worked 146 walks in 1957 compared to Williams'
119. Not to mention the standings, where the Yankees topped the second-place White
Sox by eight games, and Williams' Red Sox by 16.

Mantle was never one to shy away from nightlife, and the 1957 campaign had its
share of bumps and bruises for the Yankees on and off the field. Still, Mantle remained
one of the toughest outs, day in and day out, in 1957 and for seasons to come. Said
Williams years later: "Mantle was the greatest switch-hitter this game will ever see."

| HR | RBI | AVG | HITS | OBP |
|----|-----|------|------|------|
| 34 | 94 | .365 | 173 | .512 |

| HR | RBI | AVG | SB |
|----|-----|-----|-----|
| 28 | 61 | .325 | 65 |

# chapter 6

# THIEVES

*Speed puts pressure on a defense. With a fast batter at the plate, corner infielders have to creep in to guard against the bunt. Suddenly, no grounder is routine. And if the speedster gets on base, the defense has all kinds of new responsibilities. Some of the game's most menacing offensive stars have used their speed to wreak such havoc. During MVP campaigns, they've racked up gaudy stolen base totals. But even more importantly, day after day, they've made life for their opponents extremely difficult. As they say, speed never goes into a slump.*

## RICKEY HENDERSON  1990 (AL)

ON MAY 9, 1990, WITH HIS ATHLETICS TRAILING THE Yankees, 1-0, in the eighth inning, Rickey Henderson did his thing.

He started with a one-out double. By definition, a great base runner has to be on base to do damage, and Henderson, perhaps the all-time greatest of base runners, could get on in so many different ways (see his .439 OBP in 1990 including 97 walks). With Carney Lansford at the plate, Henderson broke for third base. A master thief, he would finish the 1990 campaign with 65 steals and the AL MVP Award. But on this play, Henderson wouldn't have the chance to tally a stolen base, as Lansford grounded a routine ball to shortstop Alvaro Espinoza.

But after seeing that Espinoza's throw to first was a soft one, Henderson accelerated into another gear. And by the time the ball reached Yankees first baseman Don Mattingly, it was too late. Henderson's headfirst slide beat the relay throw to home plate, tying the game. Oakland would win in the 11th when Henderson drew a bases-loaded walk. "I'd pay to see him play," teammate Walt Weiss said.

Several weeks later, when Toronto's David Wells fell behind Lansford, 2-0, Henderson broke from second base and stole third. With the theft, he passed Ty Cobb for the career AL lead in stolen bases. In May 1991, he passed Hall of Famer Lou Brock to become the game's all-time steals leader."

HENDERSON'S GLOVES

# FRANKIE FRISCH 1931 (NL)

ALONGSIDE ACE HURLER LEFTY GROVE, ST. LOUIS second baseman Frankie Frisch won the modern-day MVP Award in 1931, its inaugural season. He would later gain fame as player-manager of the Gashouse Gang, but that year Frisch was simply a player, and quite a good one.

Known as "The Fordham Flash," Frisch took his all-around game straight from college (Fordham, of course) to the Majors. A switch-hitter, Frisch hit .311 in 518 at-bats that season, driving in 82 runs. And true to his nickname, Frisch led the National League in steals three times, including the 1931 season, when he swiped 28.

| HR | RBI | AVG | SB |
|----|-----|-----|-----|
| 4 | 82 | .311 | 28 |

His speed also made him a menace in the field, where he had tremendous range. In 129 games at second base in 1931, he made just 19 errors and turned 93 double plays.

All this despite a huge burden on Frisch to succeed in St. Louis. In 1926, the Cardinals got him with pitcher Jimmy Ring from the New York Giants in a trade for Rogers Hornsby. "Frisch handled the pressure gracefully," Bob Broeg, sportswriter and childhood Frisch fan, wrote, "and turned in a career that put him in the Hall of Fame, too." Reflected Branch Rickey, the Cardinals executive who was on the line with the trade: "Frank Frisch saved my life."

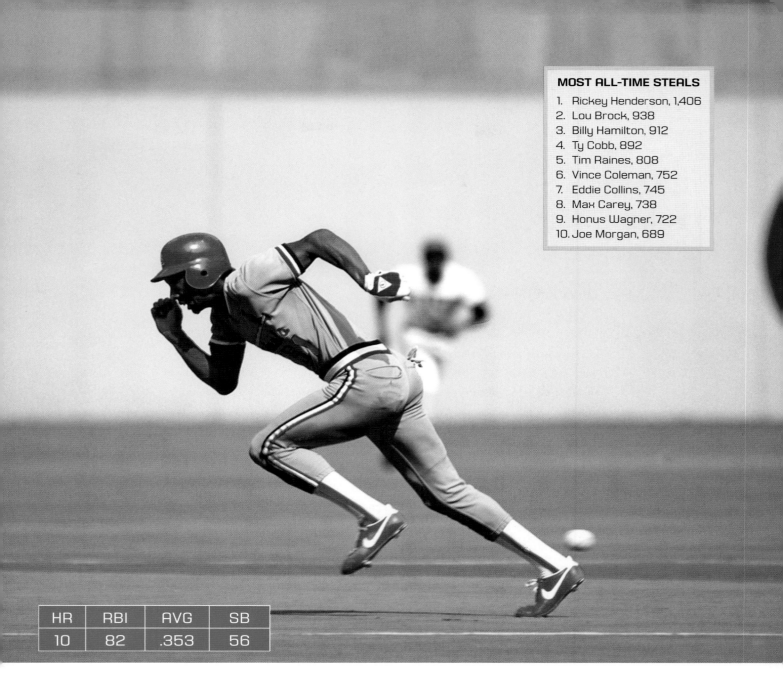

| HR | RBI | AVG | SB |
|----|-----|-----|-----|
| 10 | 82 | .353 | 56 |

## WILLIE McGEE 1985 (NL)

WILLIE McGEE WAS THE SPEEDY, SWITCH-HITTING star of St. Louis in 1985. The gifted, 26-year-old outfielder did everything for the Cards that season but win 20 games on the mound. "With the type of year he had," Manager Whitey Herzog said, "Willie should have been a unanimous choice for MVP."

McGee, who won the batting title with a .353 average and 216 hits, received just 14 of the 24 first-place votes. Not quite what his skipper wanted, but still more than enough to take the award. "He was ready to blossom," said Cardinals shortstop Ozzie Smith. "I knew the only thing that would hold him back were injuries."

McGee's legs carried him to a career-high 56 steals in 1985 and a league-leading 18 triples. Fourteen thefts came in September and October. A 7-6 loss to the Mets on Sept. 12 put the Cardinals a game behind New York. But the next day, McGee rallied his team with two steals, three runs and an RBI to beat the Cubs. They finished three games ahead of the Mets to win the NL East title.

McGee arrived in St. Louis via a 1981 trade with the Yankees. "I read about the trade in the small type in the paper," he recalled. "I called the [Cardinals] a few days later and I said: 'I think I belong to you. What are your plans for me?'" Had St. Louis answered 'NL MVP,' one might have said they were crazy.

## JOE MORGAN  1975 (NL)

IN HOUSTON'S FARM SYSTEM DURING THE EARLY 1960s, JOE MORGAN idolized Astros second baseman and future Hall of Famer Nellie Fox. "He'd talk to me every day," Morgan said, "point out little things on the field, ways I could help the team."

Those early lessons showed a decade later, as Morgan seemed to do just about everything right for the Cincinnati Reds. The club won the World Series in 1975 and 1976, and its remarkable second baseman was the NL MVP both years.

A smart runner, Morgan seemed able to take extra bases at will, yet had the restraint to hold back when the odds were against him. He swiped 67 in 1975, 60 the following season, and was only caught a combined 19 times. "I never stole a base for Joe Morgan," he later said, as Fox had taught him to steal only when the team needed it.

Morgan's speed and Pete Rose's ability to get on base fit perfectly with the power at the middle of the Reds' lineup. Morgan scored 107 runs in his first MVP effort and 113 in the next, contending for batting titles and winning a Gold Glove in each year.

Morgan went into another gear when it counted. "He was just a good Major League player when it didn't mean anything," his former Manager Sparky Anderson said. "But when it meant something, he was a Hall of Famer."

Sadly, Morgan's mentor wasn't near the field in 1975. Fox would pass away that winter from skin cancer at age 47. But he followed the progress of his protégé until the end. Morgan heard Fox was in the hospital during his first MVP campaign. "I called him," said Morgan, "and he started talking about me winning the MVP. He said he was pulling for me."

# Morgan singled in the go-ahead run in the top of the ninth in Game 7 of the 1975 World Series.

HR | RBI | AVG | SB
17 | 94 | .327 | 67

## MAURY WILLS  1962 (NL)

THE 1962 LOS ANGELES DODGERS COULD PITCH. They had Don Drysdale, who would win the Cy Young Award that season, as well as Sandy Koufax and Johnny Podres. One problem: "We didn't have any hitting," Drysdale later said.

Even if Drysdale thought they lacked power, he couldn't deny their speed. In the form of shortstop Maury Wills, speed helped the team overcome its hitting woes. "If he got on base," Drysdale said,

"stole second, Junior [Gilliam] got him to third and he scored on a sacrifice fly, we'd say heck, that's a beginning for us."

Wills spent his fair share of time on base for the Dodgers. He had 208 hits and a .347 OBP. And from there it was off to the races; he stole 104 bases (then a modern-day, single-season record) and took the NL MVP Award. The Dodgers finished second in the league in runs and second in the standings with 102 wins.

| HR | RBI | AVG | SB |
|---|---|---|---|
| 6 | 48 | .299 | 104 |

That year, Wills showed just how tough speed is to stop. When L.A. played on the rival Giants' turf in July and August, the groundskeeping crew watered the first base dirt. But the Dodgers complained and sand was dumped in the area. "The wet wasn't going to stop Wills," announcer Lon Simmons claimed, "but the sand was, or at least slow him down." But they couldn't catch him. Wills stole 12 against the Giants that season.

## BARRY LARKIN 1995 (NL)

THE CINCINNATI REDS LED THE MAJORS IN STEALS in 1995 with 190. Reggie Sanders swiped 36. Ron Gant had 23. Even football-star-turned-outfielder Deion Sanders grabbed 16 in just 33 games as a Red. But the team leader was Barry Larkin. The talented shortstop had 51 and won the NL MVP Award.

He could have padded his stats. But that wasn't Larkin's game. "I don't run just to run," he said. The 12-time All-Star ran to pressure the opposition. He ran to get into scoring position. He ran to win. Larkin was caught just five times in 1995, and the Reds won the NL Central by nine games.

He would finish with a .319 average, 98 runs and 66 RBI. And those

| HR | RBI | AVG | SB |
|---|---|---|---|
| 15 | 66 | .319 | 51 |

numbers came with Gold Glove defense. Still, there were players with better stats. Dante Bichette knocked in 128 for Colorado and hit .340 with 40 shots. Even Reggie Sanders could've made a case: 28 home runs, a .306 clip and 36 swipes.

But Larkin was a leader; his value was measured by more than individual totals. "If you look at sheer numbers, there are guys who have more homers and RBI," his then double-play partner Bret Boone said. "But it's nice to see people look at 'most valuable.' He was really great on our team. He was our leader."

# chapter 7

# FAST RISERS

*It's not every day that a rookie acclimates to the Big Leagues seamlessly. One player to have such a transition was Ryan Howard, whose debut campaign blew the NL away. As a 25-year-old in 2005, he burst onto the scene, launching 22 homers, batting .288 and driving in 63 runs in just 88 games to win the NL Rookie of the Year Award. Those stats are even more impressive considering 11 homers and 27 RBI came in September and October while he was helping the Phillies battle for the Wild Card. His team fell short, but Howard came out with more vengence in 2006, collecting 58 homers and 149 RBI, good for the MVP title. Welcome to The Show. It can't possibly be this easy …*

| HR | RBI | AVG | HITS |
|----|-----|-----|------|
| 27 | 102 | .318 | 211 |

## CAL RIPKEN JR. 1983 (AL)

ONE WOULDN'T HAVE CALLED CAL RIPKEN Jr. a grizzled vet in 1983 — the 23-year-old's second full year in the Big Leagues. But he had enough experience to know when to wait by the phone. "I knew I was going to get a phone call because of the Rookie of the Year thing last year," said Ripken, who was selected as the AL's top newcomer in 1982. "They said, 'You'll know if you get a phone call around 11 p.m.' Sure enough, the phone rang right around 11." Without even picking it up, Ripken knew he was the AL MVP.

As a sophomore, Ripken led the league in hits (211), doubles (47) and runs (121), while batting .318 with 27 homers and driving in 102 runs. And, in what would become a trend, he played in all 162 games. Thanks in large part to their young shortstop and the MVP runner-up Eddie Murray, the Orioles rolled to a World Series crown.

Murray was a key influence on the still developing Ripken, both as a mentor and as protection in the lineup. "An exceptional plus, a luxury," said Ripken, the No. 3 hitter, of having another future Hall of Famer in the No. 4 spot.

Despite his youth, Ripken's veteran teammates could not have been too surprised at his quick ascent from neophyte to MVP. His father, Cal Ripken Sr., had long been a coach in the Baltimore system. Going back to their own Minor League days, when Ripken was still a teenager, the Orioles veterans had seen what Junior could do — whether taking ground balls on the infield or ripping a few shots to the bleachers during batting practice. "I'm just playing between legends," Doug DeCinces used to say of following Brooks Robinson and holding a spot for the young Ripken on the infield.

AARON'S 1957
TEAM MVP PLAQUE

# HANK AARON 1957 (NL)

FOR A MOMENT, IT SEEMED CARDINALS center fielder Wally Moon had robbed Hank Aaron of what Aaron has deemed his most memorable home run. But Moon's leaping attempt could not bring the shot back to earth. In the 11th inning of a Sept. 23 game against the Cardinals, a 24-year-old Aaron had clinched the 1957 pennant for the Milwaukee Braves.

After floating around the bases, Aaron was carried off the field by his Braves teammates. "I think that was my biggest homer," Aaron, who would hit a then-record 755 in his 23-year career, later reflected. He would hit 44 dingers during his unforgettable fourth season. He also knocked in 132 runs and posted a .322 average during his MVP effort that year.

The Braves debuted in Wisconsin in 1953, and their 1957 win capped a magical courtship. "Baseball was at the center of Milwaukee's life — its sporting life, its cultural life," says Commissioner of Baseball Bud Selig, who, at the time, was a 23-year-old Braves diehard. At the center of it all was Aaron, who had made his own debut in 1954.

In the midst of the pandemonium that September night, Aaron thought of Bobby Thomson's home run six years earlier to clinch the pennant for the Giants. "And when I was running around the bases tonight," he told reporters after the game, "it suddenly struck me that this must be the way Thomson felt. A mighty good feeling it was, too."

| HR | RBI | AVG | SLG |
|----|-----|-----|-----|
| 44 | 132 | .322 | .600 |

MATTINGLY'S GLOVE

## DON MATTINGLY 1985 (AL)

YOGI BERRA COULDN'T EXPLAIN DON Mattingly's success in 1984. In just his second full season, the 24-year-old was locking horns with teammate Dave Winfield for the batting title. "He's one of those kids who came in and adjusted right away," said Berra, then the Yankees manager. "You don't explain it, you're just happy when it happens to somebody on your ballclub."

| HR | RBI | AVG | HITS |
|---|---|---|---|
| 35 | 145 | .324 | 211 |

After finishing three points ahead of Winfield in the 1984 batting race, Mattingly took the AL MVP Award the next season. That year New York batting coach Lou Piniella helped him add the home run to his repertoire.

"We like the way this kid sprays the ball to all fields and makes things tough on the pitcher," Piniella said.

"But over the season, a hitter is going to get a certain number of balls that he can drive for home runs, and we wanted him ready to take advantage of that situation."

Part of the adjustment was getting Mattingly to put a little more weight on his back foot. He did that on May 13, 1985, against the Twins, clearing the fences with two outs in the bottom of the ninth to give the Bronx Bombers a 9-8 win.

"I'm not afraid to let Lou tinker," Mattingly said. "He makes my body do things I can't get it to do." Mattingly would finish with a career-high 35 dingers in 1985, not to mention 145 RBI and a .324 average. The player who had Berra at a loss for words would need no adjustment period.

## FRED LYNN  1975 (AL)

BOSTON'S FRED LYNN WAS TECH-nically still considered a rookie at the start of the 1975 season, with just 43 at-bats and 18 hits on his Major League resume. Thus, he was far from a household name. With a remarkable freshman season, though, Lynn suddenly found himself on the map.

His most memorable game in 1975 came on June 18 against the Detroit Tigers, when the outfielder went 5 for 6 with three home runs, 10 RBI and a then-record-tying 16 total bases.

Thanks in part to 21 homers and 47 doubles, the 23-year-old would finish tops in the AL in slugging (.566), the first rookie ever to lead the league in that stat. He also hit .331, put up a .401 on-base clip and scored 103 runs on his way to Rookie of the Year and MVP honors.

Lynn was not the only newcomer to stand out on the Red Sox that season. Jim Rice, who later would win the 1978 MVP Award, also made his debut. Together, they gave the team a youthful spark like few rookie tandems in history, as the Red Sox rolled to the AL pennant. Rice, though, was hit by a pitch on his hand late in the year and missed the entire postseason, including Boston's memorable 1975 World Series loss to Cincinnati.

Still, it had been quite a rookie season for Lynn. "He was like a musician who brought the house down with his first number," wrote *The Boston Globe*, "or a golfer who stepped to the first tee and nailed a hole-in-one."

| HR | RBI | AVG | SLG |
|----|-----|-----|-----|
| 21 | 105 | .331 | .566 |

| SAME YEAR ROOKIE OF THE YEAR & MVP WINNERS | | |
|---|---|---|
| PLAYER | YEAR | TEAM |
| Fred Lynn | 1975 | Boston Red Sox |
| Ichiro Suzuki | 2001 | Seattle Mariners |

## VIDA BLUE 1971 (AL)

"I WISH EVERY ATHLETE, MALE AND FEMALE, YOUNG and old, could experience a year like I had," Vida Blue said. In 1971, Blue experienced what few Big Leaguers ever do, let alone those in their first full season as a starter. His wicked heater was making Little Leaguers of the game's best.

Blue lost his first start that year, but proceeded to win his next 10 decisions and 16 of his next 17. He would finish 24-8, with a miniscule 1.82 ERA and 301 Ks. "To be out there on the mound and have the confidence to know that you can throw the ball past anyone," Blue said. "To know that the hitter knows what you're going to throw and you're still throwing it by him. That's what that year was like." He won both the AL Cy Young and MVP awards.

In 1969 and '70, Blue had pitched in 18 games and won just three despite showing a flash of potential with a no-hitter late in 1970. He showed a lot more than that during the first half of 1971, proclaiming his arrival by throwing three innings for a win at the All-Star Game in Detroit. Despite his first-half success, he was star-struck by his teammates. "You could just go around the room, man," Blue said. "And I was the little ol' guy there from Mansfield, La., named Vida Blue. What the hell?"

| W | L | ERA | SO | IP |
|---|---|-----|-----|-------|
| 24 | 8 | 1.82 | 301 | 312.0 |

| HR | RBI | AVG | SLG |
|----|-----|-----|-----|
| 34 | 130 | .321 | .559 |

## JUSTIN MORNEAU
## 2006 (AL)

THE TURNAROUND IN JUSTIN Morneau's 2006 season came during an early June series in Seattle when Twins Manager Ron Gardenhire called his 25-year-old slugger in for a meeting. At that point, Morneau, a young Canadian first baseman with all kinds of potential, was hitting below .240 and his Twins were 11.5 games out of first place. "There was a lot of stuff going on off the field that didn't need to be," Morneau would admit after the meeting. "My focus wasn't what it needed to be."

With renewed attention, Morneau began his ascent. In the next game against Baltimore he went 2 for 4 with two home runs and five RBI. Off the field, Morneau adopted a more laid-back routine, featuring more time at home with his roommate, catcher Joe Mauer, and less time enjoying the nightlife.

The results followed. Morneau would hit .364 the rest of the season, finishing at .321 with 34 home runs and 130 RBI, catapulting the Twins to the top of the AL Central. When it came time to choose an MVP, the voters gave Morneau a slight edge over the Yankees' captain, Derek Jeter, who had a career year in the Bronx.

Morneau joined Larry Walker and became the second Canadian to receive the league's top honor. "To be put next to, in my opinion, a guy who should be in the Hall of Fame and is the greatest Canadian position player that's ever played — it's a real honor," Morneau said.

### HANK GREENBERG 1935 (AL)

FROM THE DAY HE ARRIVED IN DETROIT, HANK GREENBERG LOOKED the part of the imposing slugger. Often the largest player on the diamond, the future Hall of Famer's prodigious power rivaled any of the game's greats.

As one of the sport's first Jewish stars, Greenberg was often the subject of taunts, but such things didn't seem to hurt his focus at the plate. Greenberg had a historic third season, reaching 103 RBI by the All-Star break. He would finish with an American League-best 170 as well as a .328 average, 36 homers and the unanimous MVP.

Although Greenberg was "one of the finest gentleman," according to writer Red Smith, he would not back down from anti-Semitism. "He was a big guy, don't forget," his son, Steve Greenberg, once said, "6-feet-4, 220 pounds — and he challenged people if they went over the line."

In 1935, the 24-year-old anchored a terrific Tigers team,

| HR | RBI | AVG | SLG |
|----|-----|------|------|
| 36 | 170 | .328 | .628 |

which also featured second baseman Charlie Gehringer and catcher Mickey Cochrane. Together, they defeated the Cubs in six games for the team's first-ever World Series title.

Greenberg earned a second MVP nod before turning 30, after rapping 150 RBI and batting .340 in 1940. But like many of his contemporaries, he later lost a number of his prime years to military service during World War II.

In 1947, the final year of his great career, Greenberg witnessed the debut of Jackie Robinson. And with memories of the taunts he heard during the hostile 1935 Series fresh in his mind, he offered the Dodgers' pioneer encouragement. "Dad always said he thought he had it tough," Steve Greenberg recalled, "until he saw Jackie Robinson."

In addition to driving in 170 runs in 1935, Greenberg finished third in the league with 121 runs scored.

| W | L | ERA | CG |
|---|---|-----|-----|
| 24 | 7 | 2.48 | 27 |

## BOBBY SHANTZ
## 1952 (AL)

AT FIRST GLANCE, IT SEEMED A historic mismatch: The Philadelphia Athletics' puny, 5-foot-6 hurler Bobby Shantz from Pottstown, Pa., against Yogi Berra, Mickey Mantle and the rest of the Yankees' powerful hitters. But in 1952, 26-year-old Shantz was more Goliath than David. And on May 30, he willed the A's to a 2-1 victory over the Bronx Bombers, hurling 14 spectacular innings. "I must have thrown 300 pitches in that game," he recalled, "and I was 139 pounds. We didn't count pitches back then and didn't have good relief pitching. So you stayed in."

Shantz threw 27 complete games in 33 starts for Philadelphia in 1952. He would finish 24-7 with a 2.48 ERA — numbers certainly worthy of the AL MVP Award.

While he didn't have overpowering stuff (he guessed that he threw about 85 mph), Shantz had command of every one of his pitches. "To be successful as a pitcher," former A's catcher Joe Astroth later said, "you've got to throw strikes, and he could do that." With his quickness, Shantz was also a top-notch fielder. The Gold Glove Award began in 1957, and Shantz won the first eight before retiring in 1964.

Unfortunately for Shantz, he was never able to duplicate his MVP effort.

On Opening Day in 1953, while batting against Walt Masterson of the Washington Senators, Shantz was hit by a pitch and broke his left wrist. As a result he would be plagued by shoulder problems for the rest of his career.

| HR | RBI | AVG | SLG |
|----|-----|-----|-----|
| 25 | 118 | .301 | .504 |

## JEFF BURROUGHS   1974 (AL)

BEFORE JEFF BURROUGHS EVEN PUT ON HIS BIG LEAGUE THREADS, expectations were high. At one tryout, he wowed talent evaluators with a mammoth home run over the center-field fence. "He's the best 18-year-old hitter I've ever seen," said Senators Manager Ted Williams. Thanks in part to that impression, the Senators made Burroughs their top 1969 draft selection.

By 1974, thanks to a move west in 1972, the Washington Senators had become the Texas Rangers and the 23-year-old Burroughs was ready to fulfill the expectations surrounding him. Making themselves right at home in the Lone Star State, the Rangers finished second in the AL West and nearly swept the Junior Circuit hardware that year. Burroughs won the MVP Award, while teammate Mike Hargrove took the Rookie of the Year honor (although he was more than a year older than Burroughs), skipper Billy Martin won Manager of the Year and hurler Fergie Jenkins finished a close second to Catfish Hunter in the Cy Young race.

Even surrounded by such talented teammates, Burroughs was the star of the show that season. He started the campaign hitting cleanup, and true to that spot, he belted 16 home runs and knocked in 73 in the first half. The surge enabled Burroughs to become the first Ranger to start in an All-Star Game. He would finish with a team-high 25 dingers, a .301 average and 118 RBI.

| HR | RBI | AVG | SLG |
|----|-----|------|------|
| 58 | 149 | .313 | .659 |

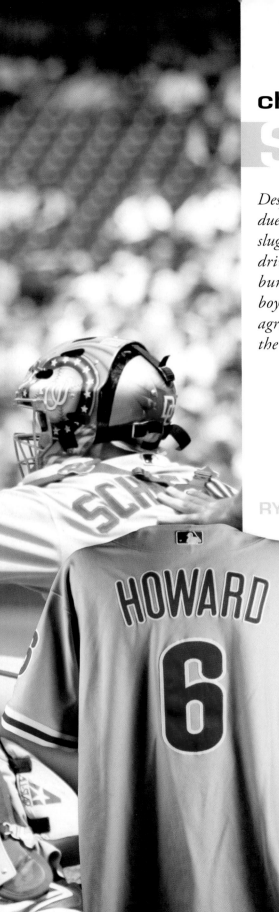

## chapter 8
# SLUGGERS

*Despite the beauty of small ball, of line-drive base hits and pitchers' duels, there's something special about the home run. "To me," the great slugger Harmon Killebrew said, "it's the ultimate in baseball — to drive the ball out of the park." Fans might clap for a well-timed bunt, but they line up during batting practice to watch the big boys pepper the bleachers. Most fans — and players — would agree that a tape-measure blast is among the most exciting plays in the game, and these MVPs sure contributed to the thrill.*

## RYAN HOWARD 2006 (NL)

IN HIGH SCHOOL, RYAN HOWARD WOULD DENT THE WALLS in his basement, where his father had built him a batting net, fit with a tee and a soft-toss machine. Howard would spend hours down there, unleashing his powerful swing and rattling the entire house. It wasn't the last home's foundation he would shake, either.

As a rookie with the Phillies in 2005, Howard began a nationwide demolition. He belted 22 homers in just 312 at-bats, taking Rookie of the Year honors. The following season, he won the MVP Award with an eye-popping 58 blasts and 149 RBI. "The first thing that came to mind," said Howard, "when I stopped and reflected on it was: 'Did this really just happen? Did I really hit 58 home runs? Did I really have the season that I just had?' It kind of hit me all at once." Now he knows how the rest of the league must have felt.

Howard entered the 2006 All-Star break with 28 home runs, tied for second in the NL behind fellow first baseman Albert Pujols, and made a statement by winning that year's Home Run Derby at Pittsburgh's PNC Park.

Howard's torrent continued in the second half, as he pummeled another 30 dingers and hit at a .355 clip. "He keeps me up after 10 at night," said Phillies Hall of Famer Mike Schmidt. "I used to go to bed after the fourth or fifth inning, but now I gotta stay up and watch his next at-bat." The MVP voters must have felt the same way, giving Howard the title over Pujols.

Thanks in part to his dingers, Maris led the league with 132 runs scored in 1961.

| HR | RBI | AVG | SLG |
|----|-----|-----|-----|
| 61 | 142 | .269 | .620 |

## ROGER MARIS 1961 (AL)

THESE DAYS, ROGER MARIS'S LEGENDARY 1961 season is finally getting its deserved recognition. But it wasn't always that way. In his prime, Maris seemed *too* talented for his own good.

That year, Maris boldly challenged a pair of pin-stripe legends — Babe Ruth and Mickey Mantle. Ruth, who hit 60 longballs during a 154-game 1927 campaign, still held the single-season home run record. Mantle was the fan-favorite, and making a run of his own at Ruth's mark. To Maris, it seemed like no one outside the Yankees clubhouse was rooting for him to win the race — which he did with 61 home runs.

But Maris wasn't trying to outdo the Babe. "I told people all season in 1961," Maris said 20 years later,

"that I didn't care if I broke the record or not, that all I was interested in was helping the Yankees get into the World Series." And Maris's 61 home runs and 142 RBI earned him his second straight AL MVP Award, as he helped New York to a world title over Cincinnati.

Still, there was noticeable anti-Maris sentiment in the Bronx. "He really didn't care one way or the other," his father, Rudy, would say of Roger and the record. "But I remember a lot of New York people resented the fact that he and not Mantle broke Ruth's record."

Maris's final homer — his 61st of the year — came in the last regular-season game, off Boston's Tracy Stallard. Many insisted the new record was tainted, as Ruth had reached his total within a shorter schedule.

**AL ROSEN 1953 (AL)**

A LETHAL POWER HITTER, CLEVELAND'S AL ROSEN was also capable of tremendous grace. After he was unanimously selected as the AL MVP in 1953, Rosen sat down and wrote a thank-you letter to every sportswriter who had cast a ballot.

Their support was well warranted. Rosen had set the club record with 43 homers, notched 145 RBI and nearly won the AL Triple Crown, falling .001 percentage points behind Washington's Mickey Vernon in the batting race (.336 to .337). "I was leading most of the season," Vernon later recalled. "But Al got hot and started getting two

| HR | RBI | AVG | SLG |
|----|-----|-----|-----|
| 43 | 145 | .336 | .613 |

or three hits in nearly every game for the last two weeks."

Rosen was so sharp toward the end that he had the batting crown in his sights on the final day of the season. After riding his powerful stroke to second place in the standings, Rosen's teammates were determined to get him the Triple Crown. Late in the contest, he still needed one more hit to pass Vernon. And thanks to a walk to teammate Joe Ginsberg in the ninth, Rosen got one last at-bat. He almost had it, too, as he nearly beat out a slow grounder to third baseman Gerry Priddy, but was called out by the umpire. His teammates would swear he was safe and Manager Al Lopez came out to argue. But Rosen would have none of it.

**GEORGE FOSTER 1977 (NL)**

IT WASN'T JUST THAT GEORGE FOSTER, THE REDS' slugger, nicknamed "Foster the Launcher" by his manager, Sparky Anderson, cleared fences with stunning ease in 1977. "I don't think I've seen the ball jump off anyone's bat like it did his," said Cincinnati's radio play-by-play man Marty Brennaman.

The Launcher tallied 52 shots in his MVP season, leading the Reds like few could have imagined during his earlier years

| HR | RBI | AVG | SLG |
|----|-----|------|------|
| 52 | 149 | .320 | .631 |

as a part-timer in San Francisco and the Queen City. "They don't make bats long enough to swing from the dugout," he said.

Foster played outfield for the Reds in the mid-1970s after Pete Rose's move to third. Fresh off his finest campaign (1976), his 29 homers in the first half of the 1977 season left sportswriters guessing how high he would go. "I don't project in that fashion," Foster countered. "Goals and guideposts sometimes get in the way."

He hit 20 in the final two months to cross the half-century mark and became the first Major Leaguer to do so in 12 years. He also finished at .320, the fourth-best average in the league, with 149 RBI, 31 doubles and 124 runs.

Anderson's only complaint: He could stand to become a truly complete player by stealing more bases. Foster countered: "I'd rather hit the ball out of the park and keep my uniform clean."

### SAME YEAR BATTING CHAMPIONS & MVP WINNERS

Charlie Gehringer, 1937
Ernie Lombardi, 1938
Jimmie Foxx, 1933, 1938
Joe DiMaggio, 1939
Stan Musial, 1943, 1948
Dick Groat, 1960
Joe Torre, 1971
Pete Rose, 1973
Rod Carew, 1977
Dave Parker, 1978
Keith Hernandez, 1979
George Brett, 1980
Willie McGee, 1985
Terry Pendleton, 1991
Ichiro Suzuki, 2001
Barry Bonds, 2002, 2004

GRIFFEY'S CAP

## KEN GRIFFEY JR. 1997 (AL)

KEN GRIFFEY SR. SAW MANY MVP SEASONS
during his career. He played 147 games in the outfield for the
Reds in 1977, when George Foster torched the NL. He also shared a locker
room with Pete Rose and Joe Morgan in their award-winning seasons. "What I recall
most of all about all their years," Griffey Sr., a three-time All-Star, later said, "was the real
joy they experienced doing the things they did to help the team."

That sort of joy flowed from his son, Ken Griffey Jr., throughout the 1997 campaign.
With his smooth-as-silk left-handed stroke and his graceful Gold Glove defense, the
Seattle center fielder played with a skill and gracefulness few of his contemporaries could
match. As a hitter, Junior most resembled Hall of Famer Stan Musial, his father would say.
"It's a great compliment to be compared to Kenny," Musial responded.

As a slugger in 1997, Griffey was often measured against Roger Maris. By June, he
had 24 home runs in 53 games, including six upper-deck shots. "See it, hit it," Griffey
said of his approach at the plate during the run. He would finish the season just five
short of the Yankees' slugger with 56, adding a .304 average, 147 RBI and another Gold
Glove Award — his eighth. The Mariners finished with 925 runs, tops in the Majors,
and 90 wins, tops in the AL West, but they fell to the Orioles in the Division Series.

Junior was still rewarded as a unanimous choice for the AL MVP Award. "I am without
a doubt the happiest old man in the world," his father said, after the announcement.
"Winning the MVP is a special thing. I know how special because I tried with all my
might and ability to be worthy of one." Junior certainly proved himself more than worthy.

| HR | RBI | AVG | SLG |
|----|-----|------|------|
| 56 | 147 | .304 | .646 |

KLEIN'S MVP TROPHY

## CHUCK KLEIN 1932 (NL)

FOR DECADES, THE KNOCK ON CHUCK KLEIN WAS that he called the Baker Bowl home for much of his career. "It was felt that Lady Godiva could hit .334 with 27 home runs in that chummy playground," wrote *The New York Times* years later.

Klein was, by all counts, a far more accomplished hitter than Lady Godiva, particularly in 1932 when he took the NL MVP Award with 38 homers, a .348 average and 152 runs scored. After that, no NL star would reach 150 runs until Jeff Bagwell in 2000.

Klein was not an imposing slugger. In fact, freckle-faced, weighing in at about 185 pounds and standing at just 6 feet, he

| HR | RBI | AVG | SLG |
|----|-----|------|------|
| 38 | 137 | .348 | .646 |

looked more like the team's batboy than a Hall of Famer. Still, Klein consistently provided oversized output for Philadelphia.

But it often went for naught, as the Phillies struggled to win games. In 1932, they finished fourth in the NL, at 78-76 (their only season in the '30s above .500). But that didn't stop voters from recognizing the slugger come award time.

That recognition is one reason, argues baseball statistician Bill James, that Klein's career should not be discounted. "He was one of those players, like Richie Allen," wrote James, "who was always the focus of attention wherever he went."

| HR | RBI | AVG | SLG |
|----|-----|-----|-----|
| 47 | 125 | .291 | .635 |

## KEVIN MITCHELL 1989 (NL)

FAIR OR UNFAIR, ANY GIANTS OUTFIELDER VYING for the MVP Award is bound to be compared with *the* Giants outfielder, Willie Mays. Kevin Mitchell held up his end pretty well in 1989, in power numbers anyway. Mitchell belted 47 homers in his MVP season, the most by a Giant since Mays hit 52 in his award-winning 1965 effort. "I talk with Mays a lot," Mitchell said. "He tells me what I'm doing wrong."

There couldn't have been too much to say in 1989, Mitchell's finest season as a Big Leaguer. He reached the century mark in runs and RBI for the first time (100 and 125, respectively), put up a .388 OBP and cranked 34 doubles. Mitchell did it with

consistency, too, batting at least .274 with six home runs in each full month of the campaign.

Mitchell's running mate throughout his five-year stint with the Giants was Will Clark, the smooth-swinging first baseman who batted third to Mitchell's clean-up in 1989. Clark hit .333 with 23 homers and 111 RBI, finishing second in the MVP race.

But Mitchell's toughness impressed voters. "If he broke his arm," wrote the *San Francisco Chronicle*, "he'd tape it between innings and go right on playing, saying it was a slight strain."

Mitchell and Clark led the Giants to a 92-70 record, taking the NL West — the franchise's first pennant since the days of Mays.

| HR | RBI | AVG | SLG |
|----|-----|------|------|
| 49 | 140 | .276 | .584 |

## HARMON KILLEBREW
## 1969 (AL)

HARMON KILLEBREW WAS NOT always a prolific home run hitter. When he broke into the Bigs in the mid-'50s, his swing was suited for line drives. But Hall of Famer Ralph Kiner approached him. "He told me that I should be hitting for power," Killebrew recalled, "and that I needed to move up on the plate and pull the ball."

It wasn't long before those line drives were regularly clearing fences. Killebrew retired in 1975 with 573 career shots, including 49 during his 1969 MVP season (a total that led to Killebrew's sixth home run crown). Between July 2 and the end of the season alone, he belted 31 homers.

Killebrew posted a career-high 140 RBI and led the league with a .427 OBP thanks to 145 walks. But Killebrew, ever the gentleman, quickly deflected the credit. "Look at that lineup," he exclaimed years later, speaking of a group that featured Rod Carew, Tony Oliva and Cesar Tovar. "I had 140 runs batted in," said Killebrew, "and I felt like I should have had about 240."

He hadn't always been so content in Minnesota. When he was a young player getting settled in Washington, the Senators moved to the Midwest. Having experienced the Twin Cities in the Minors, he had dealt with the region's chill. "I can't say I was real excited about moving," he later admitted.

But fans embraced him and Killebrew grew to like the place. "Pretty much right away," he said, "I started hitting the ball good, and I loved the fans because they're down-to-earth Midwestern people."

| HR | RBI | AVG | SLG |
|----|-----|-----|-----|
| 46 | 139 | .315 | .600 |

## JIM RICE 1978 (AL)

IN HIS HEYDAY, BOSTON'S JIM RICE WAS HAILED AS baseball's most intimidating hitter. A short, efficient cut was all he needed to drive the ball with frightening force. Physically he was also perhaps the strongest player of the era, despite claims that he had never lifted a weight.

As with many of history's great sluggers, opponents claimed the ball made a different sound off his bat, and they would line up to watch, and perhaps listen to, him take batting practice. One afternoon many believe he hit 16 in a row out of Fenway Park.

He could do it come nightfall, too. "Like most great athletes, Jim hates situations where he is out of control," said Baltimore coach Jim Frey, who managed Rice in winter ball in Venezuela. "He wants to dominate the pitcher, dictate to him." In 1978, his best season, he hit 46 home runs and knocked in 139 for the Red Sox to win the MVP Award. He also hit .315, rapped 213 hits and became the first American League slugger since Joe DiMaggio in 1937 with more than 400 total bases (Rice had 406).

That season, opponents tried everything to get back some control. Take Kansas City skipper Whitey Herzog, who pulled a four-outfielder shift out of his hat against Rice at Fenway. "What I'd really like to do," Herzog said, "is put two guys on top of the Citgo sign and two in the net."

| HR | RBI | AVG | SLG |
|----|-----|-----|-----|
| 45 | 110 | .319 | .633 |

## CHIPPER JONES 1999 (NL)

THE KEY TO CHIPPER JONES' 1999 MVP CANDIDACY was September. His Atlanta Braves entered the month with a 3.5-game lead over the New York Mets in the NL East. Jones was in the midst of a great second half, with 11 home runs in July and 10 more in August, as well as an average hovering around .320.

But Atlanta needed more to secure the division. And, as MVPs are known to do, Jones delivered the best way he knew how: with the longball. He would hit 10 in September. In a key three-game series with New York late in the month, he belted four to lead Atlanta to a sweep. The switch-hitter homered from both sides of the plate in one game, Nos. 42 and 43 on the season.

Jones hadn't always been so versatile. In 1998, Manager Bobby Cox recalled that Jones "just didn't have the power from the right side." But hitting coach Don Baylor encouraged the third baseman to attack more as a right-hander. "Don said I'm batting No. 3 and I should act like a No. 3 hitter," Jones recalled.

He would total 45 homers in the three-hole in 1999, hit .319 and drive in 110 runs. "He learns from his previous at-bat," teammate Brian Jordan said. "He keeps that book in his mind of how that particular guy pitches to him." Jones also raked 41 doubles on the year, walked 126 times and scored 116 runs as Atlanta eventually took the division by 6.5 games.

| HR | RBI | AVG | SLG |
|----|-----|-----|-----|
| 49 | 137 | .287 | .568 |

## ANDRE DAWSON
## 1987 (NL)

PRIOR TO 1987, ANDRE DAWSON was a free agent, having spent 11 years as an outfielder for the Montreal Expos. And he had a good idea of where he wanted to go. He and his agent gave the Chicago Cubs a signed, blank contract and asked General Manager Dallas Green to write in the amount. Green offered him $500,000 guaranteed, with incentives that could make the deal worth $700,000. "I took a chance," said the 1987 NL MVP, "and it worked out the best for everyone."

It worked out particularly well for Cubs fans, who fell in love with "the Hawk," as Dawson was affectionately called. "Some guys just fit in with a certain city," noted Atlanta Manager Chuck Tanner.

Although the Cubs struggled to hang in the pennant chase that summer, Dawson performed brilliantly. He homered in all three games of an early May series against the Padres at Wrigley. One month later, he put up back-to-back two-homer games. And then he belted 15 more in August, breaking a club record held by both Hack Wilson and Ernie Banks.

Come September, the only question regarding the MVP was the Cubs' record. No player from a last-place team, where Chicago was destined to finish, had ever won the award. But Wrigley fans cast their unofficial vote prior to Dawson's last home at-bat. With "M-V-P!" chants ringing in his ears, Dawson belted another over the ivy.

He would finish with 49 and 137 RBI, good enough for plenty of official votes.

## GEORGE BELL 1987 (AL)

A POWERFUL OUTFIELDER IN THE JUNIOR CIRCUIT, George Bell, the first Dominican-born player to win the MVP Award, did it all for the Toronto Blue Jays in 1987. "He's got a bad shoulder from carrying the rest of the ballclub all summer," quipped Detroit Manager Sparky Anderson.

Although the Jays eventually fell short of the postseason (to Anderson's Tigers), the left fielder had done his share to keep them in the hunt. Bell hit 47 home runs (setting a club record), including 10 in August, batted .308 and topped the AL with 134 RBI. He also piled up 16 game-winning RBI and 15 assists in the field.

| HR | RBI | AVG | SLG |
|----|-----|-----|-----|
| 47 | 134 | .308 | .605 |

Such production might have been impossible when Bell first signed in 1974, as he weighed in at 154 pounds. But after years of hard work he was 40 pounds heavier. And pitchers paid the price.

"I'm very happy," Bell said by telephone from the Dominican Republic after the voting results were made public. "Because when you win the MVP, everything shows that you've worked hard."

Although his team was knocked from contention in the final weekend by Detroit, voters recognized that had it not been for Bell's excellence throughout the year, Toronto's final series likely would have been meaningless.

# chapter 9
# RUNNERS-UP

*As fierce competitors often claim, second place is the first loser. But it's hard to pinpoint any losers in the running for baseball's highest individual honor. When it comes to the MVP Award, simply being a part of the conversation is succeeding. Hall of Famers like Bob Feller, Eddie Mathews, Al Kaline and Paul Molitor have posted incredible seasons and settled for second place. In 1978, Ron Guidry went 25-3 and finished just behind slugger Jim Rice in the voting. In 1999, Pedro Martinez whiffed 313 and won 23 games, only to come in second to Ivan Rodriguez in the final tally. Sometimes great players just pick the wrong season to have a career year.*

## DAVID ORTIZ  2005 (AL)

MUCH LIKE HIS PERSONALITY, DAVID ORTIZ'S offensive numbers for Boston in 2005 were larger than life. And similar to many great MVPs, no hitter was more feared with runners in scoring position or during late innings of a close game. "Everything changes at the plate when I go up there," Ortiz said of those pressure spots. "My mind, the way I stand, the way I see things. Everything changes. The intensity makes me change things. All I want to do is get to the ball. That's it."

He hit .352 with runners in scoring position in 2005, and .368 with two outs. In late-and-close situations (defined as the seventh inning or later, with the batting team tied, up by one or with the tying run at least on deck), Ortiz hit .346 with 11 homers in 94 plate appearances.

On Sept. 29, 2005, with the Sox one game behind the Yankees in the American League East, Boston trailed the Blue Jays, 4-3, in the eighth inning. Ortiz, who would hit 47 home runs that season and knock in 148, led off the inning with a game-tying longball. When he came to the plate again in the ninth frame, he smacked the game-winning single to score Johnny Damon, and followed it with one of his trademark ear-to-ear grins.

"We are all enormously proud of David, both on and off the field," said Boston Red Sox President and CEO Larry Lucchino at year's end. "No one has a bigger heart or a better smile."

Ortiz fell just short in the MVP vote to New York's Alex Rodriguez, as Boston did to the Yankees in the division race that season. A tough call for voters, the knock on Ortiz seemed to be his status as a DH, while Rodriguez played at third base.

## TED KLUSZEWSKI   1954 (NL)

ATHLETIC SUCCESS CAME EASY TO TED KLUSZEWSKI, CINCINNATI'S slugger who finished behind Willie Mays for 1954 NL MVP honors. The son of Polish immigrants, he had chiseled arms, honed by throwing heavy sacks at a cornstarch mill. Kluszewski was all-state in baseball, basketball and football in high school and the tight end for Indiana University, winning a Big Ten championship in 1945.

He could smash a baseball, too. In 1954, his best season, Big Klu attacked Big League pitching like he would a Purdue linebacker, roping a Big League-best 49 homers to go along with 141 RBI. Unlike most other big swingers, though, Kluszewski shortened his stroke with two strikes to make contact. Incredibly, for a guy with his power numbers, he whiffed just 35 times in '54.

| HR | RBI | AVG | SLG |
|----|-----|------|------|
| 49 | 141 | .326 | .642 |

But the Reds finished fifth in the eight-team NL that season, 23 games shy of Mays' Giants. And come voting time, New York's center fielder got the nod. Still, 1954 had been part of a great four-year stretch for Klu, establishing him as a fine hitter.

He became the Reds' hitting coach during the 1970s under Sparky Anderson. "I never heard a bad word said about him," said Pete Rose. "He was a nice man, a gentle giant."

## ALAN TRAMMELL
## 1987 (AL)

ON OCT. 3, 1987, ALAN TRAMMELL drove the Detroit Tigers to a 3-2 victory over the Toronto Blue Jays, a win that put them atop the division. In the 12th inning, with the score knotted at two and the bases loaded, he roped an RBI single through a drawn-in infield. "I would have bet anything Alan would have hit it hard," Manager Sparky Anderson said following the game.

The Detroit skipper was confident in his consistently locked-in shortstop in 1987. The previous offseason, the team's primary clean-up hitter, catcher Lance Parrish, had departed the Motor City for Philadelphia and Anderson turned to Trammell to fill the gap. "He asked me not to try and do more than I'm capable of," said Trammell, who had hit in the No. 2 spot in 1986. But, as his manager knew, Trammell was capable of plenty.

He hit .343 that season and drove in 105 runs from his new spot in the Tigers' lineup, both career highs. Trammell also belted 28 home runs, 34 doubles and scored 109 runs as Detroit took the AL East by two games over the Blue Jays.

In the American League MVP race, though, voters gave an edge to Toronto's George Bell and his 47 homers. "I've had my career year," Trammell said. "And my numbers aren't even close to Bell's."

Still, second-place numbers catapulted Detroit to the playoffs, where they fell, 4 games to 1, to the eventual World Series champion Minnesota Twins in the ALCS.

| HR | RBI | AVG | HITS |
|----|-----|-----|------|
| 28 | 105 | .343 | 205 |

## DUKE SNIDER 1955 (NL)

| HR | RBI | AVG | SLG |
|----|-----|------|------|
| 42 | 136 | .309 | .628 |

THEY STILL TALK ABOUT THE masterful stroke of the Dodgers' legendary outfielder Duke Snider. "If you put it to music," wrote Jim Murray in the *Los Angeles Times*, "it would be Beethoven. If you painted it, it would hang in the Louvre."

In 1955 the swing could be found in Brooklyn where it solidified the Dodgers' lineup. The Dodgers were the toast of the borough that season, and at the middle of it all was the Duke. With his .309 average, his 42 home runs and his 136 RBI, Snider would finish second in the MVP chase to teammate Roy Campanella. Although both received eight first-place votes, Campanella earned a slight edge.

Snider was a California boy, but Brooklyn took him as its own. Like New Yorkers, he spoke his mind, once telling fans that they didn't deserve the Dodgers. Yet they still loved him. He was family, and sweet-swinging family at that.

Campanella and Snider finished first and second in MVP voting in 1955, and the team dominated the NL and defeated the Yankees in the World Series. The Bronx Bombers had gotten the best of them in the 1941 Fall Classic, as well as in 1947, 1949, 1952 and 1953. But thanks to the Duke, 1955 was Brooklyn's year.

"We had a good balance, and I'm not just talking about ability," Snider recalled. "We were a bunch of individuals who loved each other." Campanella, Pee Wee Reese, Jackie Robinson, Don Newcombe, Gil Hodges and, of course, Snider, are forever tied to each other, to Ebbets Field — the baseball cathedral they called home — and to the borough, which adored them so.

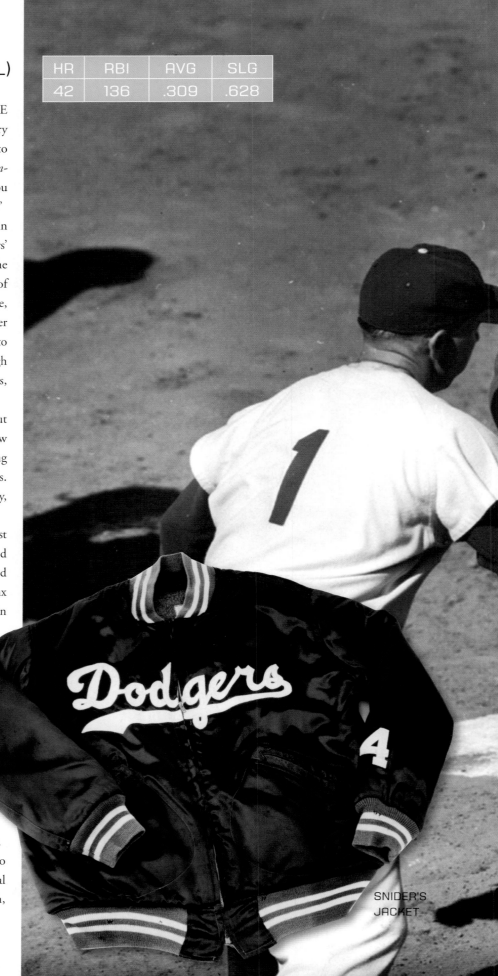

SNIDER'S JACKET

| HR | RBI | AVG | SLG |
|----|-----|-----|-----|
| 40 | 124 | .362 | .638 |

## MIKE PIAZZA 1997 (NL)

ON MAY 4, 1997, WITH A 3-0 COUNT on his teammate Jose Hernandez in the seventh inning, Chicago's Brian McRae tried to steal home. Upon reaching the plate, he found Dodgers catcher Mike Piazza, ball in tow, waiting to greet him. The collision likely filled the Los Angeles dugout with fear, as the team's star back-stop rolled in the dirt in pain. "When I saw him holding his hand," said Manager Bill Russell, "the first thing I thought was that he was going to be out a month." Piazza returned to bat in the bottom of the inning, and laced a single for his second hit of the game.

That Piazza was able to produce so consistently in 1997, and for years to follow, while playing the sport's most strenuous position, is a testament to his toughness and ability. That season he put up MVP-caliber statistics at the dish, batting .362 on 201 hits with 40 home runs and 124 RBI, but he fell short in the vote to Larry Walker of the rival Rockies.

Piazza had been a first baseman in 1988 when the Dodgers chose him as the 1,390th draft pick, reportedly at the behest of then-Manager Tommy Lasorda, who was a close friend of Piazza's father. Piazza then flew out to Los Angeles to try out for the team, but Dodgers' scouting director Ben Wade wasn't jumping to sign him.

"If he was a catcher, would you sign him?" Lasorda asked Wade.

"Yes," Wade said.

"Then he's a catcher," Lasorda said. "Sign him."

| CONSISTENT CANDIDATES WHO NEVER WON THE MVP | |
|---|---|
| PLAYER | TOP-5 FINISHES |
| Eddie Murray | 6 |
| David Ortiz | 5 |
| Will Clark | 4 |
| Bob Feller | 4 |
| Pedro Guerrero | 4 |
| Al Kaline | 4 |
| Minnie Minoso | 4 |
| Johnny Mize | 4 |
| Mike Piazza | 4 |
| Manny Ramirez | 4 |
| Albert Belle | 3 |
| Steve Carlton | 3 |
| Cecil Cooper | 3 |
| Bill Dickey | 3 |
| Prince Fielder | 3 |
| Derek Jeter | 3 |
| Mark McGwire | 3 |
| Tony Oliva | 3 |
| Kirby Puckett | 3 |
| Gary Sheffield | 3 |
| Enos Slaughter | 3 |

# BOOG POWELL  1969 (AL)

THE 1969 SEASON HAD IN MANY WAYS BEEN A CAREER year for Boog Powell, the hard-hitting first baseman on a 109-victory, pennant-winning Orioles team. The 27-year-old had reached personal bests in home runs (37), average (.304), RBI (121), hits (162) and runs (83). And he did it between a pair of Hall of Famers, Frank and Brooks Robinson, in the batting order. During one stretch in late July, Powell homered in four of five games, pulling his average above the .300 plateau for good.

Powell had hit just .228 with two homers in the first month. But a bruised rib cage resulted in a shortened stroke, a .354

| HR | RBI | AVG | SLG |
|---|---|---|---|
| 37 | 121 | .304 | .559 |

average for May and 21 homers between June and July. Still, Harmon Killebrew came out on top during MVP voting, with his own career highs in RBI (140), walks (145) and OBP (.427). Powell's his dream season had come to a disappointing end even before the tally: Baltimore was favored over the Mets in the Fall Classic, only to fall in five games.

"Saddest moment of my baseball life was when our ballclub flew back into Baltimore after losing to the Mets," he later recalled, "and 5,000 people showed up at the airport. Our fans cried, and I cried."tIn 1970, Powell bounced back taking the AL MVP, and Baltimore topped Cincinnati in the Fall Classic.

| HR | RBI | AVG | SLG |
|----|-----|-----|-----|
| 28 | 139 | .363 | .595 |

## MAGGLIO ORDONEZ
## 2007 (AL)

WITH THREE HITS IN THE FINAL game of the 2007 season, Detroit Tigers outfielder Magglio Ordonez clinched the AL batting title at .363. It was his first, and the first by a Tiger since Norm Cash in 1961. Afterward, Manager Jim Leyland inscribed a baseball for Ordonez: "The best single-season performance I've ever seen." But to voters, Alex Rodriguez was better, batting .314 with 54 home runs.

Still, it had been quite a campaign for the slugger, with 139 RBI and a league-leading 54 doubles to go with the .363 average.

Credit for the surge would go in part to his health. After missing much of the 2004 and 2005 seasons with injuries, Ordonez was in prime condition again in 2006, and even better come 2007. "I worked out really hard this offseason," he said during the onset of his 2007 season. "I felt good from the beginning of Spring Training. I said to myself, 'You're going to have a good year.'"

Detroit's spacious Comerica Park helped, too, despite its reputation as a hitter's nightmare. Ordonez hit .389 at home and belted 17 of his 28 homers there. "It's a good place to hit," he said. "You can use the gaps. It's a doubles park, a base-hit park."

Despite Ordonez's offense, Detroit fell eight games shy of Cleveland in the AL Central and lost out to Rodriguez's Yankees for the Wild Card. But to his teammates, there was no doubt Ordonez was MVP material. "I think maybe," said Ivan Rodriguez, "they should just give two this year."

| HR | RBI | AVG | HITS |
|----|-----|-----|------|
| 19 | 110 | .329 | 210 |

## KIRBY PUCKETT  1992 (AL)

THE LASTING IMAGE OF KIRBY PUCKETT'S HALL OF FAME CAREER is the excited fist pump that followed his game-winning home run in the 11th-inning of Game 6 of the 1991 World Series.

Momentum from the shot seemed to carry into the 1992 season, when the face of the Twins started on a tear. Hitting third in the order, Puckett went 2 for 5 on Opening Day with another, although more muted, home run. The fun-loving and always-hustling Puckett would hit .307 in the first month and .374 in the second. On June 3, he belted a grand slam off Toronto's Juan Guzman, his second in six days, garnering a standing ovation. "It must be my week," Puckett shrugged. He would finish with 210 hits and 313 total bases, both tops in the AL, and win his sixth Gold Glove.

But unlike 1991, the 1992 season did not end with October glory for Puckett and the Minnesota Twins. They finished second to Dennis Eckersley and the Oakland A's in the AL West, and voters gave the dominant Eck a nod in the MVP race.

At the end of the season, the Twins calmed a nervous clubhouse and fan base by signing free-agent Puckett to a new contract featuring a well-earned raise. Although an eye disease cut his career short, "his enthusiasm," recalled pitcher Bert Blyleven, "rubbed off on all his teammates, including me."

# chapter 10
# LIGHTS OUT

*Their methods were different. Some fooled hitters with breaking pitches. Some scared hitters off the plate. Others borrowed the tools of veteran teammates. But the results were ultimately the same: These MVP hurlers put up zeroes on the scoreboard. Pitching as a reliever for the Phillies in 1950, Jim Konstanty had such success. Thanks largely to a slider and a palmball, he won 16 games, posted a 2.66 ERA and he locked up a league-leading 22 saves to win the National League Most Valuable Player Award.*

## BOB GIBSON 1968

| W | L | ERA | SO |
|----|----|------|-----|
| 22 | 9 | 1.12 | 268 |

CUBS OUTFIELDER BILLY WILLIAMS CALLED it "Gibbyitis," an affliction that haunted right-handed hitters in 1968. Players facing Cardinals ace Bob Gibson suddenly had themselves scratched from the lineup. Hard to blame them. "Gibson was a tough guy out there on that mound," Williams recalled. "No hitter knew him. He looked at you like you were trying to take bread off his table."

Those who actually didn't come down with a case of "Gibbyitis" often paid a hefty price. An 0 for 4 was a common occurrence, usually accompanied by some foolish-looking swings. That's because the St. Louis right-hander was as dominant that season as any hurler in Big League history. He won 22 games, posted a ridiculous 1.12 ERA — a record for a campaign with 300 or more innings pitched — and won the Cy Young and MVP awards.

In June and July, Gibson started 12 games and won them all, allowing six runs total. In Game 1 of the World Series, he struck out 17 in a complete-game, 4-0 win.

"It was a good feeling," Gibson later said about his effect on the opposition, "showing up at the ballpark and knowing the hitters were saying to themselves, 'Damn it, Gibson's pitching today.'" As for that intense stare Williams described, Gibson said he was often just looking at the catcher's mitt. "I didn't see myself as intimidating when I was pitching," he insisted.

Nonetheless, the league certainly recognized his success. Following the 1968 season, a campaign that was dominated by pitching (including Denny McLain, Don Drysdale, Juan Marichal and, most of all, Gibson), baseball shrunk the strike zone and lowered the pitching mound from 15 to 10 inches. It was an attempt, one could say, to cure the game's hitters.

| W | L | ERA | SO |
|---|---|------|-----|
| 9 | 3 | 1.92 | 112 |

## WILLIE HERNANDEZ
## 1984 (AL)

IN MARCH OF 1984, THE PHILLIES dealt relief pitcher Willie Hernandez to the Detroit Tigers as part of a four-player deal. But Hernandez's new manager, Sparky Anderson, already knew what he was getting. He had placed a call to his former first baseman, Tony Perez, who played with Hernandez in 1983, and learned all about just how valuable the left-handed hurler was in Philadelphia.

The night of the swap, Hernandez dialed up his new skipper from Spring Training. "He told me he liked to pitch a lot," Anderson recalled, "and I told him, 'You came to the right house and knocked on the right door.'"

Once inside, Hernandez appeared in 80 games for Detroit, totaling 140.1 magical innings. With an intense scowl on the mound, he saved 32 of 33 opportunities, won nine games and posted a career-best 1.92 ERA. "I call him in, give him the ball, and shake his hand after he closes them down," Anderson said.

Credit for his success could go to a pair of pitches. Hernandez learned one, the screwball, from former Baltimore hurler Mike Cuellar during his time playing in Puerto Rico. "I was hanging my change-up, and he told me the screwball was a better pitch," Hernandez recalled. Some time later, his then-teammate with the Chicago Cubs, the future Hall of Famer Ferguson Jenkins, enlightened him on the ways of the cut fastball. "All of a sudden," Hernandez said, "I could pitch inside."

## JUSTIN VERLANDER 2011 (AL)

JUSTIN VERLANDER'S 2011 SEASON NEEDED A TURNAROUND IN the worst way. The Tigers' veteran ace began the year in sluggish fashion, going 2-3 in his first seven starts with an uncharacteristically high 3.75 ERA. The notion of his being in the running for a Cy Young Award — as he had been in years past — seemed like a dim prospect; the possibility of his becoming the first starting pitcher in a quarter-century to take home MVP honors was a pipe dream.

But Verlander made his eighth start one for the books, tossing a masterful no-hitter against the Blue Jays on May 7. "Whenever he needs to, he can hit 100 mph," said Toronto catcher J.P. Arencibia. "He's one of the more special guys on the mound."

| W | L | ERA | SO |
|----|----|------|-----|
| 24 | 5 | 2.40 | 250 |

The no-no kick-started the final five months of Verlander's 2011 MVP season, a stretch that featured the most dominant starting pitching in years. Verlander went 22-2 with a 2.08 ERA in his final 27 starts. The fireballer, known for his bewildering endurance in an age marked by fastidious concern over pitch counts, led the American League in ERA (2.40), strikeouts (250) and innings pitched (251.0), tossing no fewer than six complete innings in each of his Major League–leading 34 starts.

| W | L | ERA | SV |
|---|---|-----|----|
| 7 | 1 | 1.91 | 51 |

### DENNIS ECKERSLEY 1992 (AL)

OCT. 3, 1992, WAS OAKLAND A's CLOSER Dennis Eckersley's 38th birthday, but he wasn't happy. The night before, facing the Brewers, he had blown a save. It didn't matter that Oakland had already locked up the AL West or that it was just his third blown save in 54 chances that year. Eckersley didn't get to be so dominant — putting together an MVP season — by accepting even the most insignificant failure. "I couldn't sleep last night," he would say. "Not at all."

Devastated by each wasted pitch and middling outing, he had to remind himself of how much he truly loved baseball, of how it felt in 1989 when an injury kept him off the mound for six weeks. "I am striving for that inner peace," he admitted, "but I

haven't found it yet." Although he would often pitch one inning every night or so, closing was a 24-hour job for Eckersley. He strove for perfection.

In 1992, he was so close. He threw 80 innings for Oakland, going 7-1 and posting 51 saves. He struck out 93, walked just 11 and had a 1.91 ERA. Still, Eckersley wasn't about to toot his own horn. "I'm not cool to think I deserve an MVP," he said.

But the voters thought so. They gave him 15 first-place votes and the nod ahead of Minnesota's Kirby Puckett and Toronto's Joe Carter. "I didn't expect it," he later said, "even though I was by the phone. I didn't want to get my hopes up. I had a defense mechanism built in. It's like I don't know how to celebrate."

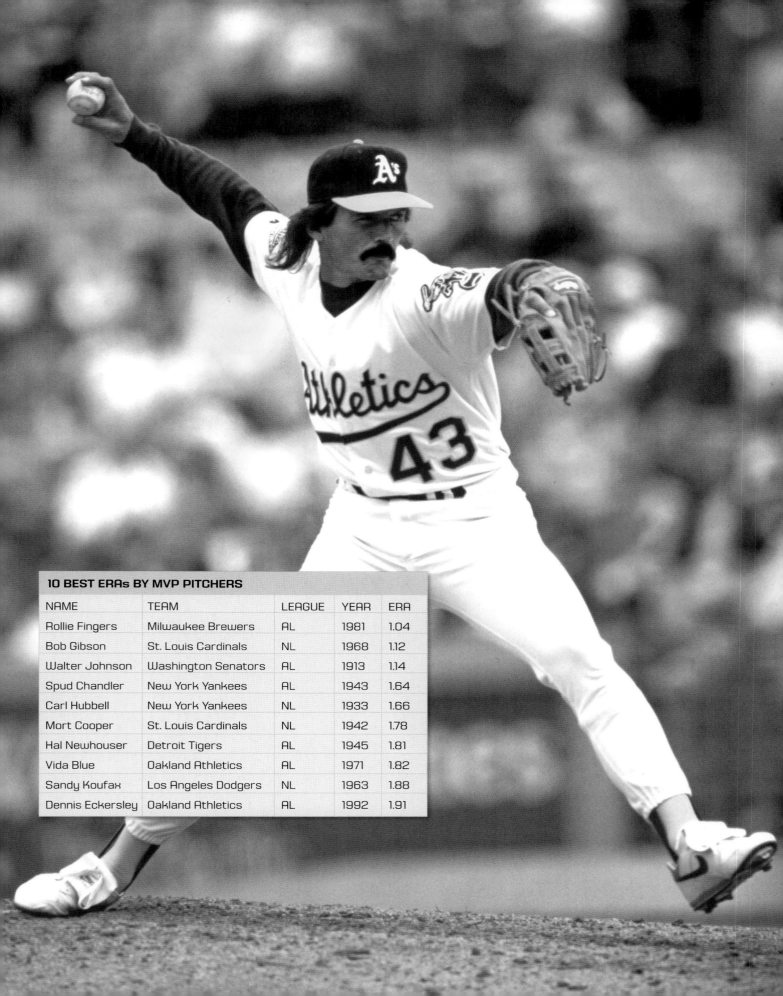

## 10 BEST ERAs BY MVP PITCHERS

| NAME | TEAM | LEAGUE | YEAR | ERA |
|------|------|--------|------|-----|
| Rollie Fingers | Milwaukee Brewers | AL | 1981 | 1.04 |
| Bob Gibson | St. Louis Cardinals | NL | 1968 | 1.12 |
| Walter Johnson | Washington Senators | AL | 1913 | 1.14 |
| Spud Chandler | New York Yankees | AL | 1943 | 1.64 |
| Carl Hubbell | New York Yankees | NL | 1933 | 1.66 |
| Mort Cooper | St. Louis Cardinals | NL | 1942 | 1.78 |
| Hal Newhouser | Detroit Tigers | AL | 1945 | 1.81 |
| Vida Blue | Oakland Athletics | AL | 1971 | 1.82 |
| Sandy Koufax | Los Angeles Dodgers | NL | 1963 | 1.88 |
| Dennis Eckersley | Oakland Athletics | AL | 1992 | 1.91 |

| HR | RBI | AVG | SB |
|----|-----|-----|----|
| 16 | 124 | .342 | 37 |

# chapter 11
# PIONEERS

*"A lot of kids looked up to him as an idol," Frank Robinson, a true pioneer in his own right, once said of Roberto Clemente, "because of the way he carried himself on and off the field, and how he gave them an opportunity to dream." Like a number of the game's courageous stars, Clemente used his tremendous baseball ability to break down barriers, often in the face of prejudice, and generally under immense pressure to succeed. Such MVPs displayed remarkable grit and integrity. These are just a few of the heroic bunch.*

## JACKIE ROBINSON 1949 (NL)

"A LIFE IS NOT IMPORTANT EXCEPT IN THE IMPACT IT HAS ON OTHER lives," Jackie Robinson famously said. And there is no doubting the positive effect his life had on so many. With great courage, years before *Brown v. Board of Education* integrated public schools, Martin Luther King delivered his "I Have a Dream" speech or Rosa Parks refused to give up her seat on a Montgomery, Ala., bus, Robinson broke baseball's color barrier as a member of Branch Rickey's 1947 Brooklyn Dodgers.

In doing so, he was under unimaginable pressure. "Jackie was my hero," Leonard Coleman, former president of the NL, once reflected. "He was my champion. He carried my every hope, my every aspiration, on his broad shoulders."

Prior to his debut, some questioned whether Robinson had the physical gifts to succeed between the lines. "Some baseball experts … even doubt he will make the Montreal (farm) club this year," wrote *Look* magazine in March 1946. But despite all the obstacles he faced, Robinson was declared Rookie of the Year in 1947 and two years later, after what would be his finest statistical campaign, was honored as the NL MVP.

He did just about everything well for the Dodgers in 1949, reaching career highs at the plate and playing stellar defense at second base. With a .342 average, he captured the batting title. Robinson also drove in 124 runs, rapped 66 extra-base hits and swiped 37 bases for first-place Brooklyn. He struck out just 27 times that season.

"Jackie established himself quickly," teammate Carl Erskine later recalled. "Around the league, he heard a lot of insults, but opponents saw fairly quickly that this guy could play."

| HR | RBI | AVG | HITS |
|----|-----|-----|------|
| 33 | 108 | .325 | 164 |

## ELSTON HOWARD
## 1963 (AL)

THOSE WHO KNEW ELSTON Howard, the first African-American to play for the New York Yankees, describe him as a man of great integrity. "Everybody in baseball respected the guy," former Manager Dick Howser said.

Like Jackie Robinson before him, Howard faced segregation and racism. During Spring Training in 1954, seven years after Robinson's debut, Howard was turned away from the team hotel in St. Petersburg because of his skin color. When the Yankees gave him a chance to establish himself as a Big Leaguer in 1955, he took advantage, batting .290. By 1963, Howard was a regular. He started the '63 season with a bang, belting home runs in each of the year's first two games. He would be named the AL MVP, after hitting .287 with 28 homers while catching 132 games. From his right-handed stance, he knocked in 85 runs and laced 21 doubles. And Howard's play behind the plate also earned him a Gold Glove.

Batterymate Whitey Ford remembered how somber Howard was after being swept in the '63 Series. "Talk about pride in being a Yankee," Ford said. "Nobody exemplified it better."

## ROY CAMPANELLA   1951 (NL)

ROY CAMPANELLA WAS 26 YEARS OLD when he debuted for the Brooklyn Dodgers in 1948, one year after Jackie Robinson. Baseball's color barrier had already cost him prime years, and the talented Campanella wasted little time in showing what he could do. He won his first of three MVP Awards in 1951 (the others came in 1953 and 1955), with a .325 average, 33 homers and his usual stunning play behind the dish.

As an African-American catcher, Campanella was in a unique position. As *The Boston Globe* wrote, "his job behind the plate required personal rapport as well as respect because he was the first black man to tell white pitchers what to throw and white fielders where to play." Not even the racism of the day could quiet his love for the game. "To play in the Big Leagues, you got to be a man," he once said, "but you got to have a lot of little boy in you, too."

CAMPANELLA'S SHIN GUARDS

| HR | RBI | AVG | SLG |
|----|-----|------|------|
| 28 | 85 | .287 | .528 |

| HR | RBI | AVG | HITS |
|---|---|---|---|
| 29 | 119 | .317 | 202 |

## ROBERTO CLEMENTE 1966 (NL)

FOR SUCH A TALENT, RECOGNITION DIDN'T COME easily for Roberto Clemente. After batting .314 with 94 RBI and stellar defense in 1960, he finished eighth in the NL MVP vote behind a group including three of his teammates. "If I am not the most valuable," he wondered, "why is it me they throw at all year?"

Barriers had been broken prior to his arrival in the Bigs, but prejudices remained. In 1955, for example, when the Puerto Rican Clemente debuted, his Hispanic-sounding first name was shortened to Bob. And when the sportswriters quoted him in the newspapers, they seemed to mock his speech. "I no run fast cold weather," the local print once read.

Through his grace on the diamond and the force of his personality, Clemente earned himself a respected place in the game and cleared the way for generations of future Latino players.

| MVP FIRSTS | | | |
|---|---|---|---|
| CATEGORY | PLAYER | YEAR | STATS |
| First Pitcher | Lefty Grove | 1931 | 31-4, 2.06 ERA |
| First Triple Crown winner | Jimmie Foxx | 1933 | .356 AVG, 48 HR, 163 RBI |
| First Batting Title winner | Jimmie Foxx | 1933 | .356 AVG |
| First Reliever | Jim Konstanty | 1950 | 16-7, 22 saves |
| First Cy Young winner | Don Newcombe | 1956 | 27-7, 3.06 ERA |

Recognition finally came in 1966, Clemente's 12th year, when he was named the National League's Most Valuable Player. That season, swinging his characteristically large bat often from the all-important No. 3 spot, he hit .317 with a career-high 119 RBI and 29 home runs for the third-place Pirates. And from right field, he pegged 17 baserunners and cut down countless doubles to win his sixth of 12 consecutive Gold Glove Awards.

In the MVP vote, Clemente earned an edge over Sandy Koufax and the Dodgers ace couldn't overlook Clemente's skills. When asked how one could pitch to the right fielder, Koufax said, "Roll the ball."

After his tragic death in a plane crash on New Year's Eve 1972, he became the first Latino player elected to the Hall of Fame. "He was our angel," Puerto Rican-born second baseman Roberto Alomar said, "the guy who opened a lot of doors."

# chapter 12
# CLOSE CALLS

*Following a terrific 29-win campaign, Detroit pitcher Hal Newhouser won the 1944 AL MVP Award by the skin of his teeth. His own teammate, Dizzy Trout, a right-handed innings eater who had thrown 33 complete games and won 27, actually got three more first-place votes, but Newhouser still took home the hardware. It was not the only year without a clear-cut favorite. The award's history is littered with seasons of more than one deserving candidate. What follows are some of the most memorable close finishes.*

| HR | RBI | AVG | SLG |
|----|-----|-----|-----|
| 41 | 117 | .330 | .609 |

## ALBERT PUJOLS OVER ANDRUW JONES 2005 (NL)

ON JUNE 25, 2005, ATLANTA BRAVES center fielder Andruw Jones came to bat in the ninth inning. He ended the game against the Baltimore Orioles with one swing, belting a walk-off homer.

It was just one more exclamation in what had already been a scream of a season for the slugger. "How can you really be surprised?" teammate Adam LaRoche asked. "He's hitting a homer a day and he hadn't gotten one yet." The blast was his seventh in eight games. He would finish the season with 51 homers — breaking the franchise record of 47 held by Eddie Mathews and Hank Aaron — and 128 RBI. And as a Gold Glove center fielder, he saved countless runs for his team. But despite earning 13 first-place votes for his performance in 2005, Jones finished short in the NL MVP balloting to St. Louis's Albert Pujols, who received 18 first-place votes.

Pujols himself had gotten used to second place. He finished there in the MVP chase annually from 2001 through 2004. But despite Jones's grand 2005 season, the voters agreed it was Pujols' turn.

It wasn't that the St. Louis first baseman raised his numbers dramatically that season. Realistically, they couldn't have gotten much better. He reached the .330 mark with 40-plus home runs for the third straight year and passed 115 RBI for the fifth time in five attempts. Pujols' status quo was otherworldly.

And he kept it up even though teammates Scott Rolen, Reggie Sanders and Larry Walker all missed extensive time that year due to injuries. In fact, the team still took the NL Central thanks in large part to Pujols. "Albert is the MVP," Manager Tony La Russa lobbied at the end of the year, "and with no disrespect to Andruw Jones, it's by a healthy margin."

| HR | RBI | AVG | FP |
|----|-----|-----|------|
| 20 | 97 | .315 | .997 |

## JOE DiMAGGIO OVER TED WILLIAMS 1947 (AL)

A 6-FOOT-4, 170-POUND HURLER, AL WIDMAR HAD yet to throw a Big League pitch prior to 1947. But at Red Sox Spring Training camp that year, he made a big-time friend in future Hall of Famer Ted Williams.

At the time, money was still an issue for a rookie like Widmar. But Williams couldn't let his friend go hungry. In the middle of an exhibition game, he approached the 22-year-old right-hander about post-game plans. "I'm taking you and buying you the biggest steak they have on the train," Williams declared.

But generosity didn't come back to Williams come season's end. Despite winning his second Triple Crown, the Splendid Splinter lost out to his rival, New York's Joe DiMaggio, in a historically close MVP vote. Since then, many have pointed to the ballot of writer Mel Webb, who left Williams out of his top 10.

## TOP 10 SLIMMEST MVP VOTE MARGINS

| YEAR (LEAGUE) | WINNER | TEAM | RUNNER UP | TEAM | VOTES |
|---|---|---|---|---|---|
| 1979* (NL) | Keith Hernandez | St. Louis Cardinals | Willie Stargell | Pittsburgh Pirates | 216 (10-4 first place votes) |
| 1947 (AL) | Joe DiMaggio | New York Yankees | Ted Williams | Boston Red Sox | 202-201 |
| 1944 (NL) | Marty Marion | St. Louis Cardinals | Bill Nicholson | Chicago Cubs | 190-189 |
| 1934 (AL) | Mickey Cochrane | Detroit Tigers | Charlie Gehringer | Detroit Tigers | 67-65 |
| 1937 (NL) | Joe Medwick | St. Louis Cardinals | Gabby Hartnett | Chicago Cubs | 70-68 |
| 1960 (AL) | Roger Maris | New York Yankees | Mickey Mantle | New York Yankees | 225-222 |
| 1996 (AL) | Juan Gonzalez | Texas Rangers | Alex Rodriguez | Seattle Mariners | 290-287 |
| 1937 (AL) | Charlie Gehringer | Detroit Tigers | Joe DiMaggio | New York Yankees | 78-74 |
| 1944 (AL) | Hal Newhouser | Detroit Tigers | Dizzy Trout | Detroit Tigers | 236-232 |
| 1961 (AL) | Roger Maris | New York Yankees | Mickey Mantle | New York Yankees | 202-198 |

\* co-MVPs

But baseball statistician Bill James wasn't convinced. "Williams lost that vote because only three people out of the 24-man panel thought he was the Most Valuable Player," he wrote.

DiMaggio, on the other hand, received No. 1 picks from eight voters. Statistically, he hadn't surpassed Williams in any major category, but DiMaggio was certainly no slouch in 1947. He hit an impressive .315, including 61 extra-base hits, and knocked in 97 runs to drive the Yankees to a first-place finish in the American League.

Competition between the two was nothing new. On the wings of a 1941 56-game hit streak, DiMaggio won his first MVP title. Williams, with his .406 average, finished second. But Boston's left fielder was generous when speaking about the Yankee Clipper. "DiMaggio," he famously said, "even looks good striking out."

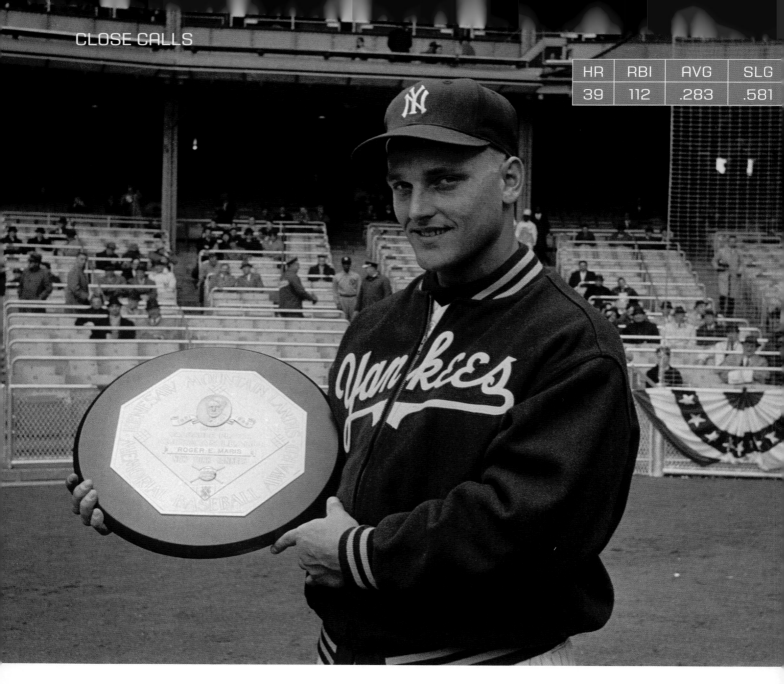

| HR | RBI | AVG | SLG |
|---|---|---|---|
| 39 | 112 | .283 | .581 |

## ROGER MARIS OVER MICKEY MANTLE 1960 (AL)

ACQUIRED FROM KANSAS CITY PRIOR TO THE 1960 season, New York's Roger Maris let his bat do the introductions. "You ask Maris a question," the slugger's new manager, Casey Stengel, said, "and he stares at you for a week before he answers." But he wasted no time with the lumber. In his first game in pinstripes Maris went 4 for 5 with two homers. He hit 27 in the first half, eliciting talk of the game's ultimate slugger, Babe Ruth.

With trademark grit, Maris slid to break up a double play late that summer and injured a muscle in his side. As a result of the injury, he finished the season with just 39 blasts. But his All-Star repertoire in right field still made him valuable to the Yankees.

Mickey Mantle was paired with Maris in the Yankees lineup. Their names would be forever linked by 1961's home run race, but they were also plenty dominant the year before.

The beloved Mantle hit 40 longballs, raked 145 hits and drew 111 walks for the first-place Yankees that season, to go along with the 94 runs he drove in.

The pair's American League MVP race was as close as their stats. Mantle, in fact, got more first-place votes than Maris (10 to 8). Ultimately, though, Maris had more overall support, and he joined his teammate (who had won the award in 1956 and 1957) as an American League MVP.

| W | L | ERA | SV |
|---|---|-----|-----|
| 6 | 3 | 1.04 | 28 |

## ROLLIE FINGERS OVER RICKEY HENDERSON 1981 (AL)

ROLLIE FINGERS CAPPED HIS unforgettable 1981 campaign with what would be one of the future Hall of Famer's most memorable strikeouts. On Oct. 3, Fingers drove the Brewers to the postseason by whiffing Detroit's Lou Whitaker, sealing a 2-1 win. It was the 61st K of the season in 78 innings of work for the Milwaukee closer, and it kicked off the team's first-ever playoff party in Wisconsin.

The Brewers, in a crucial game against the second-place Tigers, turned to Fingers in the middle of the eighth inning, down a run with Detroit's Richie Hebner on first. As he did all season, Fingers promptly closed the door, giving Milwaukee a chance to turn the tide. He would finish the year with six wins, 28 saves, a 1.04 ERA and 15 AL MVP ballots with his name at the top. "Rollie dominated that year," his teammate Jim Gantner later recalled. The MVP voters agreed. They gave Fingers a slight nod over Oakland's Rickey Henderson.

But it wasn't an easy call; Henderson was already showing signs of being one of the all-time great leadoff men in just his third Big League season. Hall of Famer Lou Brock saw it. When they met for the first time that year, Brock admitted that Henderson would break his record of 938 steals.

With great aggression, Henderson swiped 56 bags in 1981. And with great patience, he walked 64 times and reached base at a .408 clip. He would finish with 12 first-place votes, just three behind Fingers.

In 1969, McCovey was
intentionally walked a
then-record 45 times.

## WILLIE McCOVEY OVER TOM SEAVER 1969 (NL)

FOR PITCHERS IN THE 1960s, THERE WAS probably nothing scarier than the sight of Giants left-handed slugger Willie McCovey in the batter's box.

Roger Craig was one of those hurlers. Mets Manager Casey Stengel once approached his starter about how to pitch to McCovey. "Mr. Craig," Stengel inquired, "where would you like me to position the right fielder — in the upper deck or the lower deck?"

Often in 1969, McCovey's MVP season, managers saved their outfielders the trip. McCovey was walked intentionally a then-record 45 times, and 121 times in total. That he still led the league with 126 RBI, McCovey admitted, was "amazing." He also belted a league-best 45 homers, including 38 against righties.

One of those came off Mets' right-hander Tom Seaver, McCovey's main competition for the NL MVP Award. Seaver, a California native with a golden arm, was 24 and in his third season in the Big Leagues, having won 16 games in each of his first two years.

Seaver's 25 regular-season wins helped the Mets reach the playoffs for the first time. His season highlight came when he threw 8.1 perfect frames against the Cubs in

| HR | RBI | AVG | SLG |
|----|-----|-----|-----|
| 45 | 126 | .320 | .656 |

July. The next day, the New York *Daily News* labeled him "the Mets' first player stamped with greatness."

Although both players were atop 11 ballots, voters stamped McCovey the NL MVP. But Seaver might not have minded after his Mets won the World Series.

| HR | RBI | AVG | HITS |
|----|-----|------|------|
| 22 | 86 | .319 | 187 |

## TERRY PENDLETON OVER BARRY BONDS 1991 (NL)

FOR A MOMENT, ATLANTA'S TERRY PENDLETON WAS distracted. With the crowd chanting, "M-V-P!" the switch-hitter had to step out of the box. "Yeah, I did hear that," he later admitted amid a clubhouse celebration of the Braves' division title, before deflecting questions about his candidacy for the top prize.

Pendleton was named the 1991 NL MVP after winning the batting title with a .319 average, 22 homers and 34 doubles.

It's hard to believe how far the third baseman came in one season. In 1990, he played just 121 games for the Cardinals, hitting .230 with as many strikeouts as RBI (58). But Atlanta General Manager John Schuerholz took a chance on the 30-year-old, signing him to a four-year, $10.2 million free-agent deal that offseason, and it paid off. He won the MVP Award by a thin margin over Barry Bonds, who received 10 first-place votes of his own.

## MICKEY COCHRANE OVER
## CHARLIE GEHRINGER 1934 (AL)

SIMILAR TO TERRY PENDLETON, MICKEY COCHRANE changed teams prior to an MVP season. In December 1933 he moved from the Philadelphia Athletics, where he had spent the first nine years of his Hall of Fame career, to Detroit, where he would spend the remaining four.

Unlike the Braves in 1991, though, the 1934 Tigers were acquiring more than just a catcher. They were also getting a manager, as Cochrane served as both player and skipper.

The Tigers went 101-53 during Cochrane's first year, before losing to St. Louis in the World Series. At his first meeting with the team, recalled pitcher Elden Auker, Cochrane told the players "how great it was to

| HR | RBI | AVG | OBP |
|----|-----|------|------|
| 2 | 76 | .320 | .428 |

be a winner." He then went out and showed them how, hitting .320 and 32 doubles to win the MVP Award.

Challenging Cochrane in the vote was his teammate Charlie Gehringer. "Everything he did was so fluid," pitcher Hal Newhouser said of Gehringer. "It looked so easy and yet he covered so much ground." At the dish, he hit .356 and drove in 127. Still, Gehringer finished a few points behind Cochrane. Had he also served as the team's manager, Gehringer might have had a better case for MVP.

Weeks before ballots were due, Bonds suggested that a Pirate (Bobby Bonilla or himself) should win. "It's got to be that way," he asserted. Both made compelling cases. Bonilla had hit .302 with 18 homers to finish third, while Bonds had one of his monster seasons (25 homers, 43 steals, a .292 average, 116 RBI) and finished second. The loss was not a setback, though. Bonds won the next two NL MVP titles and seven overall.

## JIMMY ROLLINS OVER MATT HOLLIDAY 2007 (NL)

JIMMY ROLLINS WON THE NL MVP title with his bat, his glove and his legs, but he put himself in the conversation with his mouth. "I think we are the team to beat in the NL East," he stated prior to the 2007 season, "finally."

His words caused a ruckus in New York, where the Mets were set to defend their 2006 NL East division crown. When the Phillies arrived at Shea Stadium for the home opener in April, the Mets took two of three to drop Philly to 2-7. "I said what I said," Rollins maintained. "Our record might not show it right now, but yes, I still feel that we are the team to beat."

Then, showing that the season rests as much on endurance as anything else, he made it happen. Rollins finished with a .296 average, 30 home runs and 41 steals, winning his first Gold Glove at shortstop and helping the Phillies push their way into first place on the campaign's final day.

His main competition for the MVP Award came from the Rockies, who put on their own late-season surge.

Matt Holliday hit 21 homers in the second half for Colorado, including 12 during the final month. There was a time when Big League teams thought Holliday would choose professional football instead. But his uncle, a Rockies scout, assured the club that he might consider baseball, so the Rockies chose him with a seventh-round pick in 1998. MVP Award or no, Holliday made it worth the Rockies' while.

ROLLINS' HELMET

| HR | RBI | AVG | SB |
|----|-----|------|-----|
| 30 | 94  | .296 | 41 |

# chapter 13
# TRIPLE CROWNS

*One of baseball's rarest feats, even more so than throwing a perfect game or batting .400, is winning the Triple Crown — leading the league in batting average, home runs and RBI. Only a few of the game's greats have achieved it. After Mickey Mantle, Frank Robinson and Carl Yastrzemski all accomplished the feat within 11 years of each other (1956–67), baseball went almost half a century without a Triple Crown winner before Miguel Cabrera ended the drought in 2012. There were 13 dream seasons in the 20th century by 11 players (Ted Williams and Rogers Hornsby each did it twice), all of them future Cooperstown honorees.*

## CARL YASTRZEMSKI 1967 (AL)

THE RED SOX CONSISTENTLY FINISHED below .500 from 1961 through 1966, and the average annual attendance at Fenway Park barely topped 800,000. "Rather than a cathedral of baseball," reflected *The Boston Globe*, "Fenway was like a battered old sofa at grandma's house."

With a magical '67 season, the Boston Red Sox, in particular left fielder and future Hall of Famer Carl Yastrzemski, changed that. Fans began to believe in the team. They filled the seats and the park returned to a place of prominence. "Not only did that year bring the franchise back to life, but I think it changed the whole attitude of the Red Sox organization," Yastrzemski said. "I think the organization became winners."

Nothing contributed to this winning spirit more than Yastrzemski did down the stretch. In his final 10 games, with the pennant still in doubt, he went 20 for 37 with four homers and 14 RBI (including going 7 for 8 in the final two games). Boston won six of those contests and rolled to its first World Series appearance since 1946.

The push also helped "Yaz" win the Triple Crown with league-leading .326-44-121 totals — the first Red Sox star to achieve the feat since Ted Williams in 1947. To make it possible, Yastrzemski homered on Sept. 30 and finished tied with Harmon Killebrew in the home run race. And for his play in the outfield, which included a crucial assist on the final day of the regular season (his 13th), he won his third career Gold Glove. "With his bat, glove, arm, and will," wrote Bob Ryan, "he personified the idea of the Most Valuable Player."

For the voters, there could be no other choice. Yastrzemski received all of their first-place votes and was the runaway winner.

| HR | RBI | AVG |
|----|-----|-----|
| 44 | 121 | .326 |

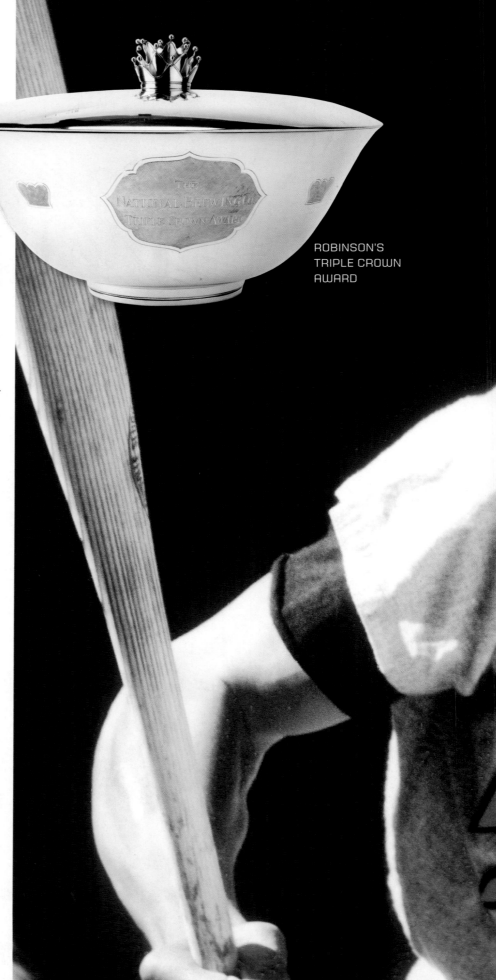

# TRIPLE CROWNS

## FRANK ROBINSON
## 1966 (AL)

IT WAS DURING A MOTHER'S DAY doubleheader against Cleveland that Frank Robinson made the loudest statement of his Triple Crown campaign with the Orioles. That day the first-year Oriole put tremendous numbers into the scorebook — going 5 for 8 with two home runs and three RBI. His second homer settled under a car in the parking lot — the first ball hit clear out of Memorial Stadium. "It started like a line drive," said Orioles left fielder Curt Blefary, "but as the ball headed into the left-field stands, it began to rise."

Thanks in part to Robinson, Baltimore took both of those games. They finished with 97 wins to lead the AL. And as was also a common occurrence in 1966, the fiery Robinson drew raucous cheers from the home crowd. When he returned to the outfield after his mammoth blast, the fans rose to their feet for a standing ovation.

At season's end, Robinson finished ahead of Minnesota's Harmon Killebrew in homers (49 to 39) and RBI (122 to 110) and just past Killebrew's teammate — Tony Oliva — in average (.316 to .307). His new team, the Orioles, would also finish nine games clear of Killebrew, Oliva and the Twins in the standings to win the AL pennant and a ticket to the World Series, where they swept the Dodgers.

Such a great season afforded Robinson a unique honor: In being named the AL MVP, he became the first to win the award in both leagues (he had won the NL MVP title with Cincinnati in 1961).

ROBINSON'S
TRIPLE CROWN
AWARD

HR | RBI | AVG
49 | 122 | .316

## JOE MEDWICK
## 1937 (NL)

DURING HIS PLAYING DAYS, JOE Medwick could be tough to get along with, his former St. Louis teammate and sometimes roommate Terry Moore once admitted. Autograph sessions with fans could result in broken pencils or thrown books. He occasionally fought teammates, too. Said Moore, "Before you even get to do enough talking to get really mad enough to fight and make a good job of it, Joe wops you and the fight's over."

Similarly, between the chalk lines there were few that could contend with Medwick, particularly in 1937 when he won the Triple Crown and the NL MVP Award.

Medwick took a high but short step with his front foot, driving anything even remotely close to the plate. He drew just 41 walks in 1937 but hit a league-best .374, belted 31 homers and knocked in 154. He also led the league in hits (237), runs (111) and doubles (56).

At the end of the '37 season, Medwick had his annual meeting with the Cards' front office, namely GM Branch Rickey, to negotiate his salary for the next year. Normally, Rickey would tell Medwick what he had done wrong during the prior campaign. "Now," quipped Medwick, on the heels of his finest effort, "I'd like to hear what you think I did wrong this year."

The team could afford to pay him for a few more seasons, but ultimately dealt him to Brooklyn in 1940.

| HR | RBI | AVG |
|----|-----|-----|
| 31 | 154 | .374 |

| HR | RBI | AVG |
|----|-----|-----|
| 44 | 139 | .330 |

## MIGUEL CABRERA 2012 (AL)

PRIOR TO 2012, MIGUEL CABRERA HAD SEPARATELY led the American League in homers (37 in 2008), RBI (126 in '10) and batting average (.344 in '11), but as the 45-year Triple Crown drought indicated, putting it all together was the tricky part. In 2012, however, Cabrera finally assembled all the pieces, becoming the first Triple Crown winner since Carl Yastrzemski in 1967 and the first Venezuela-born MVP.

From April to August, Cabrera put up MVP-worthy numbers, entering September with 33 home runs, 109 RBI and a .329 average, but a Triple Crown seemed highly improbable. That's because the Rangers' Josh Hamilton had him pegged with three more home runs and RBI apiece, and Angels rookie phenom and MVP runner-up Mike Trout had a six-point edge on the batting average leaderboard.

It was Cabrera's jaw-dropping final month that inspired his manager, Jim Leyland, to say, "I've managed a lot of players and some great ones, but I've never seen anything like this." He dazzled down the stretch with 11 home runs, 30 RBI and a .333 average in his final 31 games. On the third to last day of the season, Cabrera hit his 44th and final dinger, giving him a one-homer margin over Hamilton and a lead in all three categories. Those numbers would hold up to make him the 15th Triple Crown winner in history.

## TRIPLE CROWN WINNERS

| PLAYER (LEAGUE) | TEAM | YEAR | HR | RBI | AVG. |
|---|---|---|---|---|---|
| Tip O'Neill (AA) | St. Louis Browns | 1887 | 14 | 123 | .435 |
| Hugh Duffy (NL) | Boston Braves | 1894 | 18 | 145 | .438 |
| Nap Lajoie (AL) | Philadelphia Athletics | 1901 | 14 | 125 | .426 |
| Ty Cobb (AL) | Detroit Tigers | 1909 | 9 | 107 | .377 |
| Rogers Hornsby (NL) | St. Louis Cardinals | 1922 | 42 | 152 | .401 |
| Rogers Hornsby* (NL) | St. Louis Cardinals | 1925 | 39 | 143 | .403 |
| Jimmie Foxx* (AL) | Philadelphia Athletics | 1933 | 48 | 163 | .356 |
| Chuck Klein (NL) | Philadelphia Phillies | 1933 | 28 | 120 | .368 |
| Lou Gehrig (AL) | New York Yankees | 1934 | 49 | 165 | .363 |
| Joe Medwick* (NL) | St. Louis Cardinals | 1937 | 31 | 154 | .374 |
| Ted Williams (AL) | Boston Red Sox | 1942 | 36 | 137 | .356 |
| Ted Williams (AL) | Boston Red Sox | 1947 | 32 | 114 | .343 |
| Mickey Mantle* (AL) | New York Yankees | 1956 | 52 | 130 | .353 |
| Frank Robinson* (AL) | Baltimore Orioles | 1966 | 49 | 122 | .316 |
| Carl Yastrzemski* (AL) | Boston Red Sox | 1967 | 44 | 121 | .326 |
| Miguel Cabrera* (AL) | Detroit Tigers | 2012 | 44 | 139 | .330 |

* denotes MVP winner in Triple Crown year

## JIMMIE FOXX 1933 (AL)

WERE HE TO RISE THROUGH THE RANKS of youth sports today, baseball statistician Bill James once wrote, Jimmie Foxx would end up as a linebacker, busting through blockers to make a tackle. Said pitcher Lefty Grove: "Even his hair has muscles."

Arriving in the Bigs in 1925, Foxx was a feared power hitter and first baseman, even getting his picture on the cover of *Time* magazine in 1929. He belted 58 homers for the Philadelphia Athletics in 1932, which won him the AL MVP title. He took the award again in 1933, when his .356-48-163 offensive totals were all tops in the American League.

Foxx won the batting title that season by 20 points over Washington's noted contact hitter, Heinie Manush. He outdid Babe Ruth, to whom he was often compared, by 14 homers, and bested Lou Gehrig 163 to 139 in RBI. A true slugger, Foxx also topped Ruth in strikeouts (93 to 90) to lead the AL.

Oddly enough, Foxx had not been the only Triple Crown winner in Philadelphia in 1933. Across town, outfielder Chuck Klein, himself the 1932 NL MVP, led the NL in all three major offensive categories. But Klein's team finished 32 games under .500 and his bid for back-to-back trophies came up short.

Ironically, after the season Foxx was asked to take a pay cut due to the Great Depression. Connie Mack offered Foxx, who made $16,333 in 1933, $12,000 for the next year. They settled at $16,000.

# SOURCE NOTES

**INTRODUCTION**

6. "Chipper describes feel of hot streak" Wilkinson, Jack. "Hitting in the Jones Zone." The Atlanta Journal and Constitution 26 April 1998: 17F.

6. "Boston Globe on atmosphere in 1967" Shaughnessy, Dan. "Yaz's First Pitch was Impossible to Top." The Boston Globe 25 Oct. 2007: F7.

**CHAPTER 1**

9. "Chalmers and League Award history" Gammons, Peter. "It's Oscar Time for Baseball." Sports Illustrated 8 Sept. 1986: 22.

9. "Cobb approaches Jackson" Gutskey, Earl. "A Star is Reborn But Not Reprieved." Los Angeles Times 11 July 1989: Part 3, 3.

9. "Cobb's hands on the bat" Schwartz, Larry. "He was a pain … But a great pain." 2007. Retrieved 8 March 2008 <http://espn.go.com/sportscentury/features/00014142.html>.

9. "Cobb's swinging K's" Bak, Richard. "The Original Bad Boy." The Detroit Free Press 10 Aug. 2005.

10. "Ruth and Gehrig's personalities" Povich, Shirley. "2nd to Ruth, 2nd to Ripken." The Washington Post 6 Sept. 1995: F07.

10. "Yankees home run race" Eisenbath, Mike. "Even in Murderers' Row, Babe Ruth Stood Out As Something Special." St. Louis Post-Dispatch 8 Sept. 1998: 19.

11. "Johnson's fastball, 1913 success" Rubin, Bob. "A Farewell to Arms?" The Miami Herald 4 July 1999: 1C.

11. "James on Johnson for the losing Senators" Ryan, Bob. "Baseball 2000." The Boston Globe 31 March 2000: E7.

13. "Walker chides Ruth" Zone, Rop. "Still Only One Babe." The Seattle Times 12 Aug. 2007: D13.

13. "Ruth responds to Walker" Cava, Pete. "The Babe Provided Thrills to Indy Fans." The Indianapolis Star 10 Oct. 1999: 09C.

13. "Ruth's tough childhood" Povich, Shirley. "Legend, Truth Mix with Ruth." The Washington Post 5 Feb. 1995: D01.

13. "Ruth wants to homer in new park" Moritz, Owen. "Babe's Bat a Big Hit." The Daily News 3 Dec. 2004: 14.

13. "Ruth's first homer at new park" Maeder, Jay. "The Washup Ruth Christens Yankee Stadium." The Daily News 18 April 2003: 67.

14. "Hornsby finishes 1925 strong" Schechter, Gabriel. "Hornsby's Five-Year Batting Rampage." Feb. 19, 2007. Retrieved March 10, 2008. <http://www.baseballhalloffame.org/news/article.jsp?ymd=20070219&content_id=860&vkey=hof_news>.

14. "Hornsby avoids vice" Fimrite, Ron. "The Raging Rajah." Sports Illustrated 2 Oct. 1995: R17. 14.

14. "Hornsby second-highest paid" Sullivan, T.R. "Texas Tornado." Fort Worth Star-Telegram 19 April 1996: 10.

14. "Hornsby in as player-manager" Eisenbath, Michael. "In the Red Tradition Wasn't Hatched Immediately." St. Louis Post-Dispatch 26 April 1992: 1F.

14. "Hornsby irritates his players" Bamberger, Michael. "Hail to The Rajah." Sports Illustrated 24 June 2002: R14.

15. "Arm injury plagues Sisler" O'Neill, Dan. "The Hits Keep Coming." St. Louis Post-Dispatch 22 Sept. 2004: D01.

15. "Rickey says Sisler a professional" Eisenbath, Mike. "Sisler's Statuesque Efforts Earn Remembrance At Busch." St. Louis Post-Dispatch 17 June 2001: D8. 15.

15. "Collins says Sisler quiet" Dolgan, Bob. "Ichiro's Quest Turns Spotlight on Forgotten Sisler." Plain Dealer 15 Sept. 2004: D1.

17. "Speaker stars in Fenway opening" Globe Staff. "Moments." The Boston Globe 25 April 1995: 80.

17. "Speaker plays shallow, 1912 Series" Richards, Steve. "Speaker: First Sox Who Got Away." The Boston Globe 29 Sept. 1999: E3.

17. "Speaker born a cowboy" Dolgan, Bob. "Cowboy, Indian." Plain Dealer 12 Oct. 2005: D2.

**CHAPTER 2**

19. "Injuries slow Rodriguez" O'Brien, Kathleen. "MVP Bid A Loss Cause." Fort Worth Star-Telegram 24 Sept. 2004: 1D.

19. "Jaramillo thinks Rodriguez makes others better" Sullivan, T.R. "A-Rod American League MVP." Fort Worth Star-Telegram 18 Nov. 2003: 1A.

20. "Robinson welcomes Banks" Horn, Barry. "Baseball Hero Ernie Banks Recalls Dallas Roots." The Dallas Morning News 19 Sept. 1997: 1B.

20. "Sun-Times says Banks genuinely kind" Editorial Staff. "Banks Gets His Due, and Our Appreciation." The Chicago Sun-Times 31 March 2008: 27.

20. "Dykes on Cubs without Banks" Ernie Banks. National Baseball Hall of Fame. Retrieved 15 March 2008 <http://www.baseballhalloffame.org/hofers/detail.jsp?playerId=110533>.

21. "Hriniak cites Thomas at-bat" Krasovic, Tom. "No Doubting Thomas." The San Diego Union-Tribune 23 May 1994: D-16.

22. "Williams belts Opening Day homer" Leyden, John G. "50 Years Ago, Baseball Took A Right Turn." Plain Dealer 20 July 1996: 6D.

22. "Williams clobbers eephus pitch" Edes, Gordon. "Ted Ripped Into This One." The Boston Globe 2 April 1999: C11.

23. "Boudreau shifts Williams"; "Williams' last laugh" Leyden, John G. "50 Years Ago, Baseball Took A Right Turn." Plain Dealer 20 July 1996: 6D.

23. "Williams' streak of 84" Nowlin, Bill. "Ted Williams, 1918–2002." The Boston Globe 8 July 2002: C7.

24. "Schmidt finally at ease" Boswell, Thomas. "Mike Schmidt: the Greatest is Only Becoming Better." The Washington Post 11 March 1982: D1.

24. "Rose sees Schmidt improve" Kindred, Dave. "No One Did It Like Mike." The Sporting News 23 Jan. 1995.

25. "Kindred says Schmidt made it look easy" Kindred, Dave. "No One Did It Like Mike." The Sporting News 23 Jan. 1995.

25. "Newhouser called a 'wartime player'" Goldstein, Rich. "Hal Newhouser, 77, a Hall of Fame Pitcher." The New York Times 11 Nov. 1998: Section B, 9.

25. "Newhouser gets out of late-season jam" Guidi, Gene. "53 Years Later, Cubs' Visit Fills Newhouser's Wish." Detroit Free Press 24 June 1998: 1C.

25. "Tigers sign homegrown Newhouser" Goldstein, Rich. "Hal Newhouser, 77, a Hall of Fame Pitcher." The New York Times 11 Nov. 1998: Section B, 9.

25. "Williams admires Newhouser" White, Russ. "Prince Hal Was King for Two Years." Orlando Sentinel 2 Aug. 1992: D3.

26. "Mets cautious with Bonds" Herrmann, Mark. "Barry Carefully." Newsday 5 July 1993: 71.

26. "Stark says Bonds in his own league" Stark, Jayson. "Bonds in his own league." 15 Nov. 2004. Retrieved 16 March 2008. <http://sports.espn.go.com/mlb/columns/story?columnist=stark_jayson&id=1923229>.

28. "Yogi thinks Avila won in '54" Morning Briefing. "And Once It Was Over, Yogi Forgot About It." The Los Angeles Times 18 Sept. 1987: Part 3, 2.

28. "James says Berra's image has changed" James, Bill. The Bill James Historical Baseball Abstract. New York: Villard Books, 1986. 314.

**CHAPTER 3**

30. "Mays recalls catch against Dodgers" Stevenson, Stefan. "Willie Mays Q&A." Fort Worth Star-Telegram 18 Oct. 2007: Section D, 3.

30. "The Treiners ode to Willie Mays" The Treiners. Baseball: A Film By Ken Burns — Original Soundtrack Recording. Elektra Entertainment, 1994.

30. "No. 500 for Mays" Chronicle Staff. "Dome Moments." The Houston Chronicle 15 Sept. 1999: 3.

30. "Dark says Mays best" Sherwin, Bob. "Griffey and Mays: A New Legend Catches On." The Seattle Times 7 July 1991: C1.

33. "Alomar admires Rodriguez's 1999"; "Rodriguez throws out runners"; "Oates on Rodriguez's strong arm" Daley, Ken. "Peerless Pudge?" The Dallas Morning News 20 Feb. 2000: 24B.

34. "Rose and Stargell approach Hernandez" Boswell, Thomas. "Hernandez: Statistics, No Prize." The Washington Post 28 Sept. 1979: C1.

34. "Hernandez's great defensive stats" Post-Dispatch Staff. "Cardinals Today July 14." St. Louis Post-Dispatch 14 July 1992: 2C.

34. "Hernandez will remember race with Rose" Boswell, Thomas. "Hernandez: Statistics, No Prize." The Washington Post 28 Sept. 1979: C1.

34. "Batting crown and Gold Glove" Hummel, Rick. "Stan's in First Place." St. Louis Post-Dispatch 8 May 2005: F8.

35. "Sandberg moved to second" UPI. "Cubs Get Cey from Dodgers." The New York Times 20 Jan. 1983: Section D, 23.

35. "Frey says Sandberg could play anywhere" Ryne Sandberg. National Baseball Hall of Fame. Retrieved 17 March 2008 <http://www.baseballhalloffame.org/hofers/detail.jsp?playerId=121665>.

35. "Stone says Sandberg covers inside" McGrath, Dan. "Ryne Sandberg." Chicago Tribune 31 July 2005: Zone C, 10.

35. "Frey advises Sandberg on hitting" Elderkin, Phil. "Sandberg a Leader Among Cubs, and

the Rest of Baseball as well." Christian Science Monitor 27 Aug. 1984: 20.

36. "Hall recalls admiration of Brooks"; "Brooks a good rebounder, worked hard"; "Kell says Robinson best ever at third" Eisenberg, John. "Cornerstone at Third Base." The Baltimore Sun 7 May 2004: 1C.

38. "Bench on wear and tear" Kelly, Kevin. "Want to be a Catcher? You Had Better Be Tough." The Cincinnati Enquirer 27 July 2003: 6C.

38. "Bench's cannon arm"; "Anderson on Bench in history" Beaton, Rod. "Reds' Star Caught Fans' Attention." USA Today 10 Jan. 1989: 3C.

39. "Musial says Marion had great arm"; "Marion confident in his abilities" O'Neill, Dan. "Best Cardinals' SS?" St. Louis Post-Dispatch 4 Feb. 1992: 1B.

CHAPTER 4

40. "Kuenn bounces out to end no-hitter" Box Score from Dodgers' No-Hitter. Baseball Almanac. Retrieved 18 March 2008. <http://baseball-almanac.com/boxscore/05111963.shtml>.

40. "Berra marvels at Koufax" Sandy Koufax. National Baseball Hall of Fame. Retrieved 18 March 2008. <http://www.baseballhalloffame.org/hofers/detail.jsp?playerId=117277>.

40. "Smith on Koufax's control" Smith, Red. On Baseball. Chicago: Ivan R. Dee, 2000. 184-186.

43. "Dizzy a colorful storyteller" Gallagher, Maria. "'They X-Rayed My Head and Found Nothing.'" The New York Times 5 April 1992: Section 7, 21.

43. "Dizzy quoted after Paul's no-hitter" Bailey, Jim. "Dizzy and Paul Dean." Arkansas Democrat-Gazette 4 July 1999: C9.

43. "Dizzy's speech pattern in the booth" Etter, Jim. "Dizzy Dean Day in Spaulding to Honor Hometown Hero." Daily Oklahoman 7 Sept. 1997: 8.

44. "Hubbell's win streak in 1936" Ringo, Kyle. "King of the Screwball." Rocky Mountain News 16 July 2001: 8E.

44. "Hubbell develops screwball, says it's hard to hit" Anderson, Dave. "The Original Carl Hubbellito." The New York Times 10 May 1981: Section 5, 1.

44. "Screwball turned Hubbell around" Weil, Martin. "Giants Pitching Great Carl Hubbell, 85, Dies." The Washington Post 22 Nov. 1988: B4.

47. "Newcombe's proudest achievement was 1956 success" Dolgan, Bob. "Triumphant to Tragic." Plain Dealer 21 July 1997: 2D.

47. "Newcombe's role in Civil Rights Movement" Patterson, Kelly. "Baseball Great Portrays Struggle to Make It Big." Arlington Morning News 13 June 1998: 1A.

47. "Walters wins on TV" Staff reports. "Dustbin." The Sporting News 27 Aug. 2001: 2.

47. "Walters' move to the mound"; "Walters wishes he could've played daily" O'Neil, Dana Pennett. "Pitching to Get Grandpop Into Hall." Philadelphia Daily News 2 July 2002: 78.

48. "McLain's in-your-face style" Wolf, David. "Tiger on the Keys and the Mound." Life, 13 Sept. 1968: 79-83.

48. "McLain's injury in 1968" Guidi, Gene. "McLain May Be the Last 30-Game Winner." Pittsburgh Post-Gazette 8 Aug. 1993: D8.

48. "McLain just as busy off the field" Madden, Bill. "Cool Heat." Daily News 16 Aug. 1998: 114.

51. "Grove loses cool after loss" Steadman, John. "On Hilly Streest of Lonaconing, Native Son 'Lefty' is Still a Giant." The Baltimore Sun 22 Sept. 1996: 2C.

51. "The fate of Grove's MVP trophy" Greene, David L. "Grove's Trophy Back in Spotlight." The Baltimore Sun 21 Jan. 2001: 1B.

CHAPTER 5

53. "DiMaggio becomes aware of streak" Shuster, Rachel. "Streak that Set Standard." USA Today 9 March 1999: 4C.

53. "DiMaggio's superstitions" Gregorian, Vahe. "56 or .406?" St. Louis Post-Dispatch 14 July 1991: 3F.

53. "Breslin says DiMaggio epitomized grace" Cox News Service. "Baseball's 'Yankee Clipper' Epitomized Grace On Field and Off." Plain Dealer 9 March 1999: 1A.

55. "Brett says he's on best streak" Anderson, Dave. "Brett is Now a Happening." The New York Times 19 Aug. 1980: Section C, 11.

55. "Jackson wants to watch Brett"; "Lau says Brett a hard out" Boswell, Thomas. "Brett's Bat is Red Hot." The Washington Post 23 July 1980: D1.

55. "Chicken bows to Brett" Boswell, Thomas. "Success a Relative Matter for Bretts." The Washington Post 11 Sept. 1980: F1.

56. "Mauch says Carew not mechanically perfect"; "Carew's strong wrists, workout routine" Kindred, Dave. "Carew: .400 Year Wouldn't Change Lifestyle." The Washington Post 3 July 1977: E1.

57. "Carew's most memorable game"; "Smalley on Carew's amazing month" Reusse, Patrick. "Carew's Coronation." Star Tribune 1 July 2007: 1C.

57. "Bagwell says he can't play better" O'Connell, Jack. "Bagwell Can't Ask For More." Hartford Courant 28 Oct. 1994: C1.

57. "Unanimous MVPs"; "Biggio on Bagwell's work effort"; "Drabek says Bagwell was consistent" Hohlfeld, Neil. "Unanimous." The Houston Chronicle Oct. 28, 1994: 1.

58. "Musial develops more power" Povich, Shirley. "If Musial Could Win Batting Title at 36, Why Shouldn't Brett at 37?" The Washington Post 28 Sept. 1990: B7.

58. "Roe just walks Musial" Rubin, Bob. "Heavy Hitters." The Miami Herald 26 July 1998: 1C

60. "Torre says Ichiro can adjust" Grant, Evan. "Foreign Intrigue." The Dallas Morning News 4 June 2001: 1B.

60. "Bell on Ichiro's great start" Etkin, Jack. "Ichiro Worship." Rocky Mountain News 11 June 2001: 1E.

62. "Yount on hitting as rookie" Elderkin, Phil. "Brewer Shortstop an MVP Candidate." Christian Science Monitor 27 Aug. 1982: 16.

62. "Yount not egotistical" Leavy, Jane. "Robin Yount: Ascension Without Assumption." The Washington Post 5 March 1983: D2.

62. "Simmons says Yount uncomfortable with chant" Boswell, Thomas. "A Public Life Isn't for Super Yount." The Washington Post 19 Oct. 1982: C3.

63. "Veeck won't trade Boudreau, pays off" Pluto, Terry. "Cleveland's Favorite Son." The Seattle Times 11 Aug. 2001: D5.

63. "Veeck reflects on Boudreau's in 1948"; "Boudreau's keeps tabs on players" Jauss, Bill and Myslenski, Skip. "Much More Than a Star Athlete." Chicago Tribune 11 Aug. 2001: 8.

64. "Rose self-made, says Brinkman"; "Rose says he plays hard" "Pete Rose Just Average In Natural Ability, Makes It On Drive, Hard Work and Hustle." Associated Press (from The Los Angeles Times) 25 Aug. 1985: Part 3, 1.

66. "Gehringer quiet" Cataneo, David. "Peanuts 'N' Crackerjack." The Boston Herald 25 Jan. 1993: 74.

66. "Harris on Gehringer's hard contact" Broeg, Bob. "Consistency Marked Gehringer's Career." St. Louis Post-Dispatch 5 Feb. 1993: 8D.

67. "Phone threat to Parker"; "Parker aggressive on the field"; "Parker's boasts" Boswell, Thomas. "Parker's Deeds Matching His Words." The Washington Post 22 Sept. 1978: E1.

68. "Lackey on Guerrero's impatience" Saxon, Mark. "Zone of His Own." The Orange County Register 15 June 2004.

69. "Scioscia marvels at Guerrero" Brown, Tim. "Putting the 'V' in Valuable." Los Angeles Times 17 Nov. 2004: Part D, 1.

69. "Guerrero met Scioscia's expectations" Gonzales, Mark. "Late Run Propels Guerrero to MVP." The Arizona Republic 17 Nov. 2004: 1C.

70. "Torre still proud of 1971"; "Maxvill says Torre was great" Eisenbath, Mike. "Dream Season." St. Louis Post-Dispatch, 18 Aug. 1991: 1H.

70. "Catching wore on Torre" Mendez, Carlos. "Torre Understands Pudge's Position on Switch." Daily Oklahoman 19 April 2000.

71. "Burks on Walker away from home" Reid, Jason. "Walker Making Most of it." Los Angeles Times 20 Sept. 1997: Part C, 1.

71. "Murray says Walker not haughty" Murray, Jim. "Walker's Only Airs Are a Mile High." Los Angeles Times 21 Sept. 1997: Part C, 1.

72. "Mantle on Williams"; "Williams on Mantle" Sullivan, George. "Splendid Splinter was Idol of Yankees Legend Mickey Mantle." The Boston Herald 29 Aug. 1998: 041.

72. "James says Mantle worth of MVP" James, Bill. The Bill James Historical Baseball Abstract. New York: Villard Books, 1986. 382-383.

72. "Mantle, teammates get in trouble" Maeder, Jay. "After Hours." Daily News 7 Sept. 2003: 37.

CHAPTER 6

75. "Henderson's win over the Yankees"; "Weiss would pay to see Henderson" Liotta, Tim. Associated Press 10 May 1990.

76. "Broeg on Frisch and pressure" Broeg, Bob. "A Special Time, A Special Place and a Very Special Moment." St. Louis Post-Dispatch 22 May 2000: 15.

76. "Rickey on Frisch after trade" Barber, Red. "Baseball's Frisch-for-Hornsby as Big as Any Player Trade Ever." Christian Science Monitor 26 Aug. 1988: 18.

77. "Herzog thinks vote should be unanimous"; Smith on McGee ready to blossom" Nowell, Paul. The Associated Press 19 Nov. 1985.

77. "McGee on hearing about trade" Chicago Tribune Wires. "Cards' McGee NL Most Valuable Player." Chicago Tribune 19 Nov. 1985: Zone C, 3.

78. "Fox mentored Morgan" Bock, Hal. The Associated Press 2 Jan. 1985.

78. "Morgan stole for the team" Bass, Mike. "Morgan: Had to Work a Little Harder." St. Louis Post-Dispatch 9 Jan. 1990: 6C.

78. "Anderson on Morgan being clutch" Kay, Joe. The Associated Press 5 Aug. 1990.

78. "Morgan called Fox" Bock, Hal. The Associated Press 2 Jan. 1985.

80. "Drysdale says Wills was key" Hermann, Mark. "Wills Fills Speed Need." Newsday 28 March 1993: 12.

81. "Simmons recalls Giants tactics" Bush, David. "Putting Sand in Will's Tank." The San Francisco Chronicle 31 May 2002: C6.

81. "Larkin could've run more" Horrigan, Jeff. "Larkin Credits His Diet for Stolen-Base Acumen." Pittsburgh Post-Gazette 22 Aug. 1995: D3.

81. "Larkin deserving according to Boone" Walker, Ben. The Associated Press 16 Nov. 1995.

CHAPTER 7

82. "Ripken waits by phone"; "Murray helps young Ripken" Leavy, Jane. "Ripken Named MVP, Murray Second." The Washington Post 17 Nov. 1983: E1.

82. "Veteran Orioles remember young Ripken" Boswell, Thomas. "Young Oriole Has Been in Oriole Plan for Years." The Washington Post 3 March 1982: C1.

85. "Aaron clinches pennant, says most memorable"; "Aaron recalls Thomson homer" Haudricourt, Tom. "Aaron Pulled Off Late-Night Miracle." Milwaukee Journal Sentinel 3 July 1999: 4.

85. "Selig recalls 1957, Milwaukee's love" Vanderberg, Bob. "Living High Life." Chicago Tribune 18 July 2007: Zone C, 5.

86. "Berra can't explain Mattingly's success"; "Piniella on Mattingly's power" Elderkin, Phil. "Many Reasons for Don Mattingly's Big Year." Christian Science Monitor 17 Sept. 1984: 26.

86. "Mattingly on Piniella's help" Wolff, Craig. "Yanks, Down By 8-0, Win 9-8." The New York Times 14 May 1985: Section A, 21.

88. "Lynn's June 18 performance"; "Globe on Lynn's first season" Richards, Steve. "Lynn Shone in Golden Season." The Boston Globe 9 Oct. 1999: G6.

88. "Lynn first rookie to top slugging"; "Rice breaks hand" Herzog, Bob. "Ultimate Impact Rookies." Newsday 2 April 2006: H57.

89. "Blue wishes others could experience zone"; "Blue describes feeling on mound" Romano, John. "Looking Back on Blue Streak that Left Baseball, Fans Agog." St. Louis Post-Dispatch 1 May 1996: 4D.

89. "Blue on feeling at All-Star Game" Brown, Daniel. "All-Star Memory — Vida Blue." San Jose Mercury News 19 June 2007.

91. "Gardenhire wakes up Morneau"; "Morneau's new routine" Souhan, Jim. "Rewarding Season." Star Tribune 22 Nov. 2006: 1C.

91. "Morneau honored to be tied to Walker" Etkin, Jack. "Morneau's Fast Ascent." Rocky Mountain News 22 Nov. 2006: 10C.

92. "Smith says Greenberg a gentleman" Smith, Red. On Baseball. Chicago: Ivan R. Dee, 2000. 20-22.

92. "Son says Greenberg didn't back down"; "Greenberg encouraged Jackie, son says" Stone, Larry. "Greenberg Shouldn't Be Lost to History Books." St. Louis Post-Dispatch 6 Sept. 1998: D7.

95. "Shantz against Yanks, guesses on pitch count" Carchidi, Sam. "A's Gone, But Hardly Forgotten." The Philadelphia Inquirer 25 Sept. 2002: E01.

95. "Shantz guesses he threw 85" Cook, Bonnie L. "An Athlete and a Gentleman." The Philadelphia Inquirer 30 Sept. 2007: L03.

95. "Astroth says Shantz threw strikes"; "Shantz's broken wrist" Cook, Bonnie L. "An Athlete and a Gentleman." The Philadelphia Inquirer 30 Sept. 2007: L03.

95. "Burroughs wows Williams at tryout" Chick, Bob and Poiley, Joel. "Jeff Burroughs." Tampa Tribune 23 July 1995: 12.

95. "Burroughs first Ranger to start" Fraley, Gerry. "All-Star Flashback." The Dallas Morning News 18 June 1995: 14B.

CHAPTER 8

97. "Killebrew says homer is the ultimate" Barreiro, Dan. "It Was a Killer Run." Star Tribune 2 April 1999: 10C.

97. "Batting cage in Howard home" Goold, Derrick. "Opportunity Knocks." St. Louis Post-Dispatch 15 Jan. 2006: D10.

97. "Howard can't believe he hit 58" Strauss, Joe. "Howard the MVP." St. Louis Post-Dispatch 21 Nov. 2006: C1.

97. "Schmidt has to stay up to watch Howard" Ortiz, Jose de Jesus. "Philly Phenom." The Houston Chronicle 15 Sept. 2006: 1.

98. "Maris just wanted to help Yankees"; "Rudy Maris says Roger didn't care"; "Details of No. 61" Gutskey, Earl. "The Crowd Still Roars." Los Angeles Times 1 Oct. 1991: Part C, 1.

100. "Rosen writes thank you letters" Plain Dealer Staff. "Where Are They Now?" Plain Dealer 11 July 1999: 2C.

100. "Vernon says Rosen got hot"; "Rosen's last at-bat in 1953" Dolgan, Bob. "When Rosen Nearly Wore a Crown." Plain Dealer 12 June 2001: 1D.

100. "Anderson calls him 'Foster the Launcher'" Kindred, Dave. "The Wait Pays." The Washington Post 21 July 1977: C1.

100. "Brennaman on Foster's power" Fay, John. "He Might've Hit 70 HR Today." The Cincinnati Enquirer 22 Jan. 2003: 1B.

101. "Foster on swinging from dugout"; "Foster won't predict how many homers"; "Anderson, Foster differ on steals" Kindred, Dave. "The Wait Pays." The Washington Post 21 July 1977: C1.

103. "Griffey Sr. on MVP years" Finnigan, Bob. "Griffey Wants a Ring to Go With Trophy." The Seattle Times 13 Nov. 1997: C1.

103. "Musial honored to be compared to Junior"; "Griffey's upper deck count, hitting approach" Raley, Dan. "In Pursuit of 62." Seattle Post-Intelligencer 1 June 1997: C9.

103. "Griffey Sr. thrilled, Jr. humbled by MVP" Finnigan, Bob. "Griffey Wants a Ring to Go With Trophy." The Seattle Times 13 Nov. 1997: C1.

104. "Lady Godiva could hit in Baker"; "Klein's physical appearance" Smith, Red. "Chuck Klein of Baker Bowl." The New York Times 6 Aug. 1980: Section B, 7.

104. "James says Klein was considered great" James, Bill. The Bill James Historical Baseball Abstract. New York: Villard Books, 1986. 402.

105. "Mitchell talks to Mays" Perkins, Dave. "Kevin Mitchell Lives in His Own World." The Toronto Star 17 Oct. 1989: C4.

105. "Mitchell would play through arm injury" Cohn, Lowell. "The Best Left Fielder?" The San Francisco Chronicle 12 Oct. 1989: D1.

107. "Kiner advises Killebrew" Souhan, Jim. "Rewarding Season." Star Tribune 22 Nov. 2006: 1C.

107. "Killebrew compliments his teammates"; "Killebrew fears move but changes tune" Barreiro, Dan. "It Was a Killer Run." Star Tribune 2 April 1999: 10C.

108. "Rice says he never lifted weights"; "Rice a batting practice legend"; "Rice's total bases compare to DiMaggio"; "Herzog's shift, wants to put them on fence" Richards, Steve. "Slugger Rice Epitome of Power, Strength." The Boston Globe 10 Dec. 1999: C2.

108. "Frey says Rice needs control" Boswell, Thomas. "Rice: Talented, Dedicated, Loyal … and Often Bush." The Washington Post 20 May 1979: D4.

109. "Cox says Chipper improved from right"; "Jones recalls Baylor's advice" Kernan, Kevin. "Chipper Casts His MVP Vote." The New York Post 22 Sept. 1999: 074.

109. "Jordan on Jones' mental book" Stinson, Thomas. "Jones' MVP Stand." The Atlanta Journal and Constitution 26 Sept. 1999: 1E.

110. "Dawson's blank contract, says he took chance"; "Tanner on Dawson and Chicago" Orr, Frank. "The Hawk Soaring High Again!" The Toronto Star 30 Aug. 1987: E6.

110. "MVP chant at Wrigley" Mitchell, Fred. "'MVP!' 'MVP!' Dream Comes True for Cubs' Dawson." Chicago Tribune 19 Nov. 1987: Zone C, 1.

111. "Anderson says Bell carried Jays"; "Bell happy work paid off" Times Wire Services. "Toronto's Bell Edges Trammell in AL MVP Vote." Los Angeles Times 18 Nov. 1987: Part 3, 2.

111. "Bell's weight increase, quick bat" Justice, Richard. "The Blue Jays' Bell is Bell of the Ball." The Washington Post 24 Aug. 1987: D3.

## CHAPTER 9

113. "Ortiz on hitting under pressure" Heuschkel, David. "Putting Aside Designations." Hartford Courant 30 Sept. 2005: C6.

113. "Lucchino's proud of Ortiz" Silverman, Michael. "Ortiz Whiffs on MVP." The Boston Herald 15 Nov. 2005: 079.

114. "Kluszewski at the corn-starch mill, amateur sports"; "Rose on Kluszewski as gentle giant" Staff Reports. "Kluszewski Recalled as a 'Natural.'" The Washington Post 3 April 1988: C2.

114. "Kluszewski impresses at Indiana" Associated Press (from The New York Times) 30 March 1988: Section A, 24.

114. "Kluszewski shortens with two strikes" Olson, Stan. "Contact sport?" The Seattle Times 2 July 2001: E7.

114. "Anderson on Trammell's Oct. 3 RBI"; "Trammell marvels at Bell's numbers" Whicker, Mark. "Trammell Puts Tigers One Victory from Title." The Orange County Register 4 Oct. 1987: C01.

114. "Trammell on move to clean up" Collier, Phil. "Turning On the Tiger Offense." The San Diego Union-Tribune 9 Feb. 1988: D-1.

116. "Murray on Snider's swing"; "Snider speaks his mind" Murray, Jim. "He Sure was Artful as a Dodger." Los Angeles Times 30 Aug. 1988: Part 3, 1.

16. "Snider says 1955 team was family" Plaschke, Bill. "Boy, It's Good to See Duke." Los Angeles Times 15 Sept. 1999: Part D, 1.

118. "McRae collides with Piazza, scares Russell" News Wires. "Piazza Scares Up a Win." Buffalo News 5 May 1997: 16S.

118. "Lasorda lobbies for Piazza" Larue, Larry. "Something to Prove." Rocky Mountain News 22 June 1997: 6C.

119. "Powell's rib injury helps" Carry, Peter. "Highlight." Sports Illustrated 18 Aug. 1969. Retrieved 24 April 2008. <http://vault.sportsillustrated.cnn.com/vault/article/magazine/MAG1082731/index.htm>.

119. "Powell recalls Ryan and sting of 1969" Mizell, Hubert. "Blaster from the Past." St. Petersburg Times 11 Oct. 1990: 1C.

121. "Leyland signs baseball" Morosi, Jon Paul. "ARod Rolls Maggs for MVP." Detroit Free Press 20 Nov. 2007: 8.

121. "Ordonez finally healthy" Costello, Brian. "Magg-nificent." The New York Post 18 Aug. 2007: 53.

121. "Ordonez on Comerica" Staff Reports. "Race Still on for Maggs." Grand Rapids Press 21 Sept. 2007: D1.

121. "Pudge says they should give two MVPs" Staff Reports. "'Mates Join MVP Campaign." Grand Rapids Press 15 Sept. 2007: C3.

121. "Puckett says must be his week" Antonen, Mel. "Puckett, Twins Pull 1-3 Knockout." USA Today 4 June 1992: 4C.

121. "Blyleven recalls Puckett's enthusiasm" Kirby Puckett. National Baseball Hall of Fame. Retrieved 8 April 2008. <http://www.baseballhalloffame.org/hofers/detail.jsp?playerId=120790>.

## CHAPTER 10

122. "Williams on Gibbyitis" Kaufman, Ira. "Bob Gibson was Virtually Unhittable in 1968." Los Angeles Times 28 Feb. 1988: Part 3, 15.

122. "Gibson on his intimidation" Kramer, Staci D. "Look of a Winner." Chicago Tribune 21 Oct. 1994: 1.

125. "Calls surround Hernandez trade" Anderson, Dave. "Hardball by Hernandez." The New York Times 14 Oct. 1984: Section 5, 5.

125. "Hernandez on learning from Cuellar, Jenkins" Diaz, Jamie. "He's Giving Batters the Willies." Sports Illustrated 10 Sept. 1984: 50.

126. "Eckersley's mindset as a closer, superstitions" Ostler, Scott. "Eckersley's Saving Grace." The San Francisco Chronicle 6 Oct. 1992: C1.

126. "Eckersley says he's not cool"; "Eckersley on winning the MVP" Antonen, Mel. "Reliever Says Team Got Him There." USA Today 20 Nov. 1992: 3C.

## CHAPTER 11

129. "Frank Robinson on Clemente as an idol" Stinson, Thomas. "Hero's Dream Lives On." The Atlanta-Journal Constitution 16 April 2003: 3C.

129. "Coleman says Robinson was hero" Coleman, Leonard. "NL President Coleman Reflects on the Impact of Jackie Robinson." Los Angeles Times 13 April 1997: Part C, 1.

129. "Look writes of doubters" Telander, Rick. "A Stirring Legacy." Chicago Sun Times 15 April 2007: A85.

129. "Erskine on Jackie's quick impression" Herzog, Bob. "The Artful Dodger" Newsday 30 March 1997: H20.

130. "Campanella as first African-American catcher" Oliphant, Thomas. "The Defiant Hope of Campanella." The Boston Globe 4 July 1993: A23.

130. "Campanella on love of baseball" Anderson, Dave. "In Roy Campanella, the Heart of a Hero." The New York Times 28 June 1993: Section C, 8.

130. "Howard respected in baseball says Howser" Schumach, Murray. "Howard is Eulogized as a Man of Integrity." The New York Times 17 Dec. 1980: Section B, 7.

130. "Hotel turned Howard away" Wimbish, Ralph. "Pinstripe Pioneer." The New York Post 10 Sept. 2003: 009.

130. "Ford on Howard's Yankee pride" Schumach, Murray. "Howard is Eulogized as a Man of Integrity." The New York Times 17 Dec. 1980: Section B, 7.

132. "Clemente on 1960 MVP" Gergen, Joe. "Forgotten Pioneers." Newsday 29 March 1998: H29.

132. "Prejudice against Clemente at his debut, example in print"; "Koufax on pitching to Clemente" Wulf, Steve. "25" Sports Illustrated 19 Sept. 1994: 111.

133. "Alomar on Clemente opening doors" Stinson, Thomas. "Hero's Dream Lives On." The Atlanta-Journal Constitution 16 April 2003: 3C.

## CHAPTER 12

134. "LaRoche on Jones walk-off" Curtright, Guy. "Andruw Again." The Atlanta Journal-Constitution 26 June 2005: 1E.

134. "St. Louis injuries"; "La Russa on Pujols as deserving MVP" Miklasz, Bernie. "Pujols' stats clearly spell out 'MVP'" St. Louis Post-Dispatch 2 Oct. 2005: D1.

136. "Williams generous with rookie" Jacobsen, Steve. "The Thundering '40s." Newsday 4 April 2004: K26.

137. "James on 1947 vote" James, Bill. The Bill James Historical Baseball Abstract. New York: Villard Books, 1986. 382-383.

137. "Williams on DiMaggio" Greenberg, Paul. "Alone on the Field, DiMaggio and Williams." Arkansas-Democrat Gazette 10 July 2002: B8.

138 "Stengel on Maris not answering questions" Durso, Joseph. "Roger Maris is Dead at 51." The New York Times 15 Dec. 1985: Section 1, 52.

138. "Maris had more than power" Herzog, Bob. "Tools of the Trade." Newsday 6 Sept. 1998: C13.

139. "Fingers clinches postseason spot, Gantner quoted" Haudricourt, Tom. "Little Hits Led to Comeback Victory for 1981 Brewers." Milwaukee Journal Sentinel 15 May 1999: 6.

139. "Brock and Henderson meet" Purdy, Mark. "Henderson Finally Pleases the Crowd with Historic Steal" San Jose Mercury-News 30 April 1991: B1.

141. "Stengel on positioning outfielders"; "McCovey calls RBI total amazing" Peters, Nick. "McCovey Made Powerful Statement." Sacramento Bee 4 May 2003: C5.

141. "Daily News comments on Seaver" Hinckley, David. "Never So Close." Daily News 19 June 2003: 37.

142. "Crowd serenades Pendleton and he hears it" Wilkinson, Jack. "Pendleton Might Sit on Batting Title." The Atlanta Journal and Constitution 6 Oct. 1991: Section F, 02.

142. "Pendleton's free agency" Bodley, Hal. "Pendleton a Bold Pickup for Braves." USA Today 8 Oct. 1991: 4C.

143. "Bonds on MVP Pirates" Verducci, Tom. "You're the Best." Newsday 27 Sept. 1991: 198.

143. "Cochrane becomes Tigers skipper, meets team" Dow, Bill. "Cochrane a Good Model for Pudge." The Detroit Free Press 5 April 2004: 7E.

143. "Newhouser on Cochrane as fluid" Puscas, George. "Grace, Skill and Manner." The Houston Chronicle 24 Jan. 1993: 3.

144. "Rollins says Phillies team to beat, defends it" King, Steve. "Rollins is the Player to Heckle at Shea." The Philadelphia Daily News 10 April 2007: 69.

144. "Uncle thinks Matt might play baseball" Piecoro, Nick. "Making the Right Choice." The Arizona Republic 11 Oct. 2007: 4.

## CHAPTER 13

146. "Attendance figures, Fenway as old sofa" Ryan, Bob. "It's Impossible to Overlook 1967 Dreamers." The Boston Globe 25 Oct. 2004: C12.

146. "Yastrzemski says 1967 changed organization" Shaughnessy, Dan. "Yaz's First Pitch was Impossible to Top." The Boston Globe 25 Oct. 2007: F7.

146. "Ryan says Yaz personified Most Valuable" Ryan, Bob. "No. 10 Carl Yastrzemski." The Boston Globe 22 Dec. 1999: E1.

148. "Robinson's big home run, Blefary quote" Brown, Doug. "Outta Here." The Baltimore Sun 27 July 1995: 7C.

150. "Medwick's feisty personality, Moore quote"; "Medwick's stride at the plate" Eisenbath, Mike. "In Meeting Game, Life Head-On, 'Ducky' Always Kept 'Em Ducking." St. Louis Post-Dispatch 1 Sept. 1992: 1B.

152. "Bill James says Foxx was a linebacker" James, Bill. The Bill James Historical Baseball Abstract. New York: Villard Books, 1986. 335.

152. "Gomez on Foxx's hair muscles" Richards, Steve. "Foxx and Sox were good match." The Boston Globe 24 Nov. 1999: E2.

152. "Foxx's 58 blasts put him on *Time*"; "Foxx paid $16,000 in 1934" Dolgan, Bob. "No Fence Could Keep Foxx in the Park." Plain Dealer 15 July 1999: 3D.

152. "Foxx forced to take pay cut" Conlin, Bill. "Latest Depiction Dishonors Dignity Foxx Took to Grave." Fort Worth Star-Telegram 25 Aug. 1996: 14.

Project Statistical Research: http://www.baseball-reference.com/

Project Article Research: http://www.nexis.com/

# CREDITS

# INDEX